Rev. Henry Davis

BEYOND THE KIKUYU CURTAIN

BEYOND THE KIKUYU CURTAIN

By

H. VIRGINIA BLAKESLEE, M.D.

Missionary to Kenya under the Africa Inland Mission

MOODY PRESS
CHICAGO

Printed in the United States of America

Dedicated
to
Kikuyu martyrs
who have laid down their lives
rather than deny
the Lord of glory

PREFACE

"WHY ARE YOU GOING TO AMERICA?" asked the Kikuyu hotel boys as I waited on the hotel veranda for the bus that was to take me to the Nairobi airport.

"I am going to my country to tell my people the Agikuyu are not all Mau Mau," I replied.

The great world outside Africa has heard of the Kikuyu tribe, numbering a million and a quarter souls, who live in the highlands of Kenya Colony. It has heard, too, of Jomo Kenyatta, the instigator of the ill-famed Mau Mau secret society which has been responsible for the atrocities that have been and still are being committed in the Colony. As a result, many misinformed people have jumped to the conclusion that the Gospel has lost its power and that missionary endeavor in the Kikuyu tribe has been a failure. The purpose of this book is to correct that false impression. In making a fair appraisal of the situation, several factors must be borne in mind:

> Kikuyuland, as has every heathen domain, has been dominated by the prince of darkness for past ages.
>
> The flooding of the district with the light of the Gospel has revealed the hidden things of darkness, the character and source of every evil tribal custom.
>
> The powers of darkness have retaliated in proportion to the penetration of that Gospel light.
>
> A supernatural work of the Holy Spirit in the hearts of many Kikuyu men and women has called out from

> the tribe a Church, a part of the Body of Christ, a people persuaded that neither persecution, nor sword, nor death, nor powers, nor things present, nor things to come, can separate them from the love of Christ.
>
> The ultimate triumph of the Prince of light and destruction of the powers of darkness is foretold many times in the Scriptures and therefore is to be reckoned upon.

Over a period of more than forty years, most of it spent in close contact with the Agikuyu, I have witnessed many engagements in the titanic conflict between light and darkness in Kikuyuland. It has followed an oft-repeated pattern: First, petty clashes with the pagans and their affairs. Second, a period of growth and prosperity in spiritual work. Third, rumbling threats of the enemy. Fourth, a climax of open and organized opposition which has left the visible church decimated but purified and strengthened. In the last analysis the present Mau Mau outbreak will be seen as an all-out attack by the powers of darkness to black out forever the Light of the world in Kikuyuland.

The story of the conflict on the Kikuyu ridges, and what has led to the present crisis, I have sought to present, not as a treatise on the subject, but as a narration of incidents which have come under my personal observation and through the lives of Agikuyu with whom I have been personally associated. The gist of their conversations I have recorded as I remember them. Pertinent scenes in the depths of the villages to which I have not been an eyewitness I have reconstructed according to the well-known pattern of Kikuyuland. The Kikuyu custom of naming their children has produced many duplicate names. In several instances, people of minor importance having the same name as prominent ones have been given other suitable Kikuyu names to avoid confusion.

There has been no attempt on my part to write a history of missions in Kenya, nor even of the Mission with which I have been affiliated, nor do I lay claim to any priority as spokesman in this account. The same story, with variations as to personal experiences, might be told by any of my fellow workers whose years of faithful labor on the ridges and in the valleys have been the means of carrying the light into the darkness of Kikuyuland.

I acknowledge with thanks the help and inspiration I have received from *A Saint in Kenya,* by Mrs. Henry Scott; *Kikuyu Conflict,* by Cannon T. F. C. Bewes; *Mau Mau and the Kikuyu* and *Defeating Mau Mau,* by L. S. B. Leakey; and the lectures, *Kikuyu in Transition,* by Dr. J. W. Arthur. My debt to Miss Evelyn W. Woodsworth, of the editorial staff of *Inland Africa,* for her able and generous assistance in the preparation of the manuscript can never be repaid. My thoughts go out to my fellow missionaries of all societies in Kenya Colony and African Christians attached thereto who have been an inspiration and encouragement to me during the years spent in Kikuyuland. To all, I give thanks for the joys and happy fellowship we shared.

—H. VIRGINIA BLAKESLEE

Media, Florida, 1955.

CONTENTS

MATARA
1911-1916

CHAPTER PAGE

GITHUMU
1921, 1922

KIJABE II
1927-1937

GITHUMU
1946-1954

MATARA
1911-1916

Chapter 1

KIKUYULAND

IT WAS OCTOBER in 1911, East Africa's springtime, when the cold rains of the equatorial highlands had given place to more clement weather. The first light of a new day was breaking over the hoary wild olive trees and stately junipers about us as our caravan began to climb the almost perpendicular escarpment above the highland station of Kijabe, field headquarters for the handful of pioneer outposts in Kenya Colony that made up the Africa Inland Mission at that time. A new recruit, just arrived from the homeland, I was being escorted by a seasoned lady missionary to my assignment on a faraway post in the depths of Kikuyuland. We missionaries rode on the backs of mules, while two Kikuyu boys, Kihoga and Kamau, whose duty it was to look over the mules and protect us from danger, led the way over the steep trail. Six African porters carried boxes of provisions, clothing, camp cots, and bedding—all packed in sixty-pound loads.

When we reached the plateau above the escarpment, our path wound in and out among clumps of St.-John's-wort aglow with fragrant yellow flowers. Presently it left this pleasant plain to cross a foul-smelling marsh out of whose black mud grew scattered bunches of grass and reeds. Our boys had us get off the mules so that they could lead them around the edges of the marsh. The poor beasts often slipped from the clumps of reeds and sank to their middles only to plunge and lunge until they reached another clump where they could regain their footing. As for us, we armed ourselves with long stout staffs for support and jumped from one island of reeds to another—not without fear lest we also should be overtaken by the misfortunes of the mules.

The tropical sun was directly overhead when we left the marsh behind us and entered a bamboo forest, again on the backs of our mules. But the sun never penetrated its ceiling of waving leaves. Its shadowy floor was carpeted with trailing mosses intertwined with miniature sweet-pea vines that were bright with pink and lavendar bloom. The full-grown bamboos were six inches across at their bases and reared themselves to a height of twenty-five feet. We had been told that elephants pass through bamboo forests as men walk through grain fields.

"If you hear a crashing of bamboos," our informant had warned us, "dismount and lie flat on the ground."

We had not gone far before we began to see huge round footholes freshly made in the soft mud of the trail we were following. Then, there it was, just as we had been warned—crash! crash! crash!

"Are the elephants coming?" we cried, preparing to dismount and seek refuge in a depression.

"No," laughed the Kikuyu boys, "you hear the falling of the old bamboo poles. They have finished their life and rotted at the bottom."

As we went on, our way was obstructed constantly by bamboos that had fallen across the path. Walking ahead of us, Kihoga and Kamau would have to slash these poles with sharp knives and toss the pieces into the tangle of poles on either side of the trail before we could go on. Sometimes the boys loitered behind us. Then, if a strong pole had fallen on a level with the mule's back, the mule would take charge of the situation himself. Without waiting for the boys to come or his rider to dismount, he would duck his head under the pole and stolidly move forward. The unfortunate passenger, caught in the solar plexus by the pole, would take a toboggan slide down over the mule's tail to a safe but splashy landing in the black mud.

After traveling thus through the bamboos for an hour and a half, our caravan entered a wonderful old virgin forest. The narrow path that wound in and out around its massive trees was used by Africans as they went back and forth between the eastern and western boundaries of Kikuyuland. The day was coming when sawmills would be built around its outer edges and many of its great trees would be cut into slabs and shipped to distant parts of the world to be converted into pencils. But now it stood in all its primeval grandeur, untouched by the hand of man.

We caught our breath in delight over the new beauty that was revealed at each turn of the winding trail. Once it was an old tree. Its heart eaten out by disease and insects, it had fallen to lodge in the branches of its neighbor. In its decaying fibers the winds had planted and the rains had watered great masses of dainty ferns and dwarf pink periwinkle. Or it was the decorated stump of another forest giant. The tree that had grown on it had crumbled to become a part of the rich soil that nourished the luxuriant plants growing all about. Mosses had padded the outside of the stump, while ferns and dainty flowering vines had filled the center and draped themselves gracefully over its sides. Or we would see a vine which had festooned itself from tree to tree and from which red flowers like bells were suspended on long stems.

From time to time we caught a delicate fragrance that would disappear only to come back again as we would turn the next bend in the path. What was its source? At last we found it. It came from one of the forest begonias that had climbed up the trunk of a tree. There was nothing to identify it among the many other parasitic vines twining themselves about the forest trees, but there in the treetops it had burst, like a skyrocket, into showers of pink and white splendor.

Who could ever imagine that in forty years this vast and lovely forest would become the stronghold of the Mau Mau bands that were to spread terror over all Kikuyuland? That the atrocities which were to be committed in its shadowy depths would be published abroad in the journals of the civilized world? That the outlaws of its secret rendezvous would be hunted down with guns like rabbits?

Our winding trail turned and took us abruptly on a long, steep descent to a forest river that was dark and deep with the recent rains. The Kikuyu boys took one look at it and declared that it was impossible for the mules to cross at that point. They decided to take them downstream to look for a ford and plunged into the tangled mass of jungle vines and briers, advising us not to follow them. I walked to the water's edge and tried to determine upon a way to reach the other side. The water flowed slowly. It looked treacherous. Rocks jutted out of it here and there, but the spaces between them were wide and the stones were covered with slippery moss.

"If this river is deep enough to drown two mules, how shall I escape if I miss my footing?" I asked.

My traveling companion was lost in quiet meditations and had no suggestions to offer. While I was trying to summon up enough courage for the leap from the bank to the first rock, I looked up to see a figure emerge from the forest on the opposite bank. He was clad in the tattered remains of a red woolen blanket, two corners of which were tied with a string on his left shoulder, and he was singing one of his tribal songs to while away the hours as he journeyed over the lonely forest trail. I was having my first glimpse of a raw heathen Mugikuyu,[1] a representative of the tribe to which I was being sent.

Unconscious of another human presence anywhere about, the man was startled for an instant when he became aware of the two white women standing on the bank of the river. Then a faint smile flitted over his features as he seemed to take in the situation. In another moment he leaped from rock to rock with the grace and confidence of a deer. Reaching my side, he stretched out his hand and spoke. But the sounds he made, though punctuated with pleasant smiles, were those of an unknown tongue.

"He is saying," explained my companion, who understood him, " 'I see you are afraid. I do not wear on my feet the queer things you have on yours. They will cause you to slip on mossy rocks. Take my hand that I may help you to cross to the other side.' "

I put my hand into his strong black hand. He helped me from rock to rock—just as carefully as though I were a piece of rare old china which might shatter to a thousand bits if allowed to get a single jar—and as gallantly as though I had been a queen. Landing me safely, he dashed back to help my companion in the same way. After a "thank you" and a few remarks about the dangers of the forest rivers were exchanged between him and the missionary who knew his language, he jumped from rock to rock again and sprang up the hill to disappear in the forest depths. There that day was born in my heart a love for the Kikuyu people.

In another hour we came to a country of ridges and valleys, covered with high brachen, bushes, and scattered trees. Once these ridges, too, had been covered by the forest, before the Kikuyu tribe had advanced gradually from the northeast to take

[1] "Kikuyu" is an Anglicized form of the tribal name. The people refer to themselves as "Agikuyu" and an individual of the tribe as a "Mugikuyu."

possession of them. In the process of establishing themselves, they had cleared large areas of valuable forest, felling the trees and burning them, in order to cultivate the soil—until now Kikuyuland resembled an island surrounded on the south, west, and north by the remains of a once-magnificent virgin forest.

Kikuyu villages built on the sides and tops of the ridges began to appear. We descended a succession of deep ravines between them, at the bottom of which were rivers bridged by logs pulled into position by Kikuyu men when the waters were low. At each river we crossed, we found ourselves faced with another ridge to climb only to descend to cross another river and climb another hill. From one high point we sighted a lone shack, a part of the mission station toward which we had been traveling all day. Only one more hour of climbing ridges and crossing rivers and our journey would end. Then slowly and wearily the mules climbed the path that led up the last hill, and there before us on the summit lay Matara mission station.

The combination school and chapel had been built of redwood slabs split by hand from trees of the nearby forest. Beyond the chapel was a two-roomed house of the same material which the resident lady missionary, Miss McKinstry, was to share with me. A four-roomed house of imported lumber, bought in Nairobi and transported to this site on the backs of porters, housed the McKenrick family. There were various other buildings about the place for the use of Africans living on the station.

Our welcome at Matara was warm and genuine. Smiling Africans brought hot bath water to our rooms in a galvanized iron tub. The adventures of the journey were related to our fellow missionaries during the evening meal amid peals of laughter. The following morning every inch of my anatomy felt like a black and blue spot as I tried to rise from my camp cot, for the seldom-used muscles had felt the effects of a day on muleback, but I was ready to face the new life at Matara and begin to lay the foundaton for a missionary career.

Here first impressions soon would fade, and I would become a vital part of the life of the Agikuyu living on the surrounding ridges. I would speak their language, share their joys and sorrows, and try to help them solve their problems. Best of all, I would help to bring to them a knowledge of the light of the Gospel of Jesus Christ which had illuminated my own way and made it bright with His presence.

Chapter 2

LEARNING AN UNKNOWN TONGUE

"WE WILL HAVE our language lessons every morning at 9:30," announced Mr. McKenrick on the evening of my second day at Matara. "When we have had some lessons on the principles of the construction of this Bantu language, I will expect you to go to the villages to get acquainted with the people and listen to their conversations. I have found this the best method of getting a grasp of their language."

Bewildering lessons followed. There were no textbooks. The language had been only partially explored. But we had the notes of those who were interested in gathering material for a Kikuyu grammar, and Mr. McKenrick was considered to be one of the best linguists in the tribe. I was introduced to the ten classes of Kikuyu nouns, their agreements and disagreements. Worst of all were the verbs, with their prefixes, infixes, and suffixes. *Enda* was the stem of the verb "to love." *Ni-ndi-mu-end-ete* meant "I have loved her." But if it were any of the other nine classes of nouns that I happened to love, each one would have had a different infix.

"Oh, dear!" I sighed one day as I was struggling with the confused verb constructions. "Tomorrow I will go out to the villages and listen to their conversations. Perhaps that will help."

The next afternoon was one of those perfect blue and gold ones often seen in Kikuyuland during the long dry season. The blue vaulted sky suspended over ridges, valleys, and rivers was cloudless and laid its circle on horizons that seemed far away. Dressed in a safari suit, high laced elkskin shoes, and a pith helmet, I set out for the villages with Wambui *wa* Giciru.[1] Wambui was particularly clever in being able to understand what the white people wished to say when they had difficulty in remembering Kikuyu words. She also knew a few English words which she managed to use to good advantage in times of emergency.

"Will I ever be able to hear and speak Kikuyu?" I asked as we two walked along a winding bush path.

"You know very soon. I help you," replied Wambui encouragingly.

The path led to a large Kikuyu village, a picturesque collection of cone-shaped huts, where we found a group of women going through various processes in the preparation of corn gruel.

"*Muri ahoro* [are you with peace]?" we greeted after the usual manner.

"*Turi ahoro, no anga inyui* [we are with peace and perhaps you are]," they replied with friendly smiles.

"And who is this stranger you have brought to our village?" one of them inquired of Wambui.

"She is the *Bibi Mugeni* [the lady stranger] who has just arrived at the mission."

Wambui began to chatter to the women as they worked, talking of affairs which were of interest to them, while I sat on a three-legged stool trying to teach my ears to hear Kikuyu. Cer-

[1]Wambui of Giciru, indicating that Wambui was the daughter of Giciru. Surnames are not used among the Agikuyu, but it is customary to refer to a person as being "of So-and-so," naming the parent or owner.

tain oft-repeated words and phrases were so indelibly impressed on my mind that they would cruise through my brain for days to come, and never would be forgotten.

There was much to see as well as hear in this typical heathen village of the ridges. A Kikuyu village, I was to learn, was the home of only one family. Its owner, who achieved his status by right of inheritance or by having established the village, was highly honored and implicitly obeyed. Around his large circular *thingira* (the men's hut) where he entertained his friends and where his wives brought his food to him, were huts for each of his wives, with attached small grain huts, and similar thatched slab huts for each of his married sons and their wives or his brothers and nephews with their dependents. Here the large closely knit family would carry on its communal life, and every village was a beehive of activity as the women went about their appointed tasks of feeding and providing for the demands of their menfolk.

This afternoon two young women, nude to the waist, stood on opposite sides of a large wooden mortar alternately bringing down their long wooden pestles on the maize kernels in its hollow interior. A woman standing near them was winnowing maize, tossing it high into the air for the wind to blow away the chaff, deftly catching every grain on a wide round tray made of thin willows the cracks of which had been filled with cow dung, now dry and hard.

Another woman was kneeling by a long flat stone. A rock under the end nearest to her tilted it downward to the broad clean banana leaf which she had placed beneath the other end. One of the women at the mortar scooped out the mass of damp cracked maize and placed it on this grinding stone. Grasping a long, narrow stone, the kneeling woman began to grind. The flour that sifted down to the banana leaf she gathered up and put into a clay pot filled with water which she had in readiness. The coarse particles were removed and returned to the grindstone until all the maize was reduced to fine flour. The pot of starchy water would be taken into the hut and placed by the evening fires to ferment. The next day it would be cooked until it thickened. Hot or cold, the villagers would revel in its buttermilk-like flavor as they sipped it from dried gourd shells.

As I watched the graceful rhythmic movements of the women who were cracking the maize, I was seized with a strong desire to try my hand at the mortar and pestle. Grasping the pestle of one of the women, I motioned to them to let me have a turn. Wambui took her place opposite me with the other pestle.

"*Onei! Onei!*" shrieked the women in a burst of laughter as I brought down my pestle with a thud and made us lose the rhythm.

"*Onei, onei,*" I repeated. "What could that mean?"

"Look," replied Wambui.

"*Onei*—look," I pulled out my notebook and wrote it down.

"*Niekuria mbembe?*" the women asked Wambui.

"What is *mbembe?*"

"This *mbembe,*" said Wambui, holding up a cob of maize. Then she brought her teeth together on it with a click and added, "*Kuria mbembe,* this."

"It must mean to eat maize," I told myself. "They are asking if I eat maize. I will see if I am right when we reach home."

"This *ucuru,*" explained Wambui, pointing to the large pot of starchy water.

Ucuru went into the notebook, too. The words of the leave-taking formalities as well were jotted down, their meaning to be learned later as I went over my day's vocabulary gleanings with the *Bibi* McKinstry.

"*Tigwo na uhoro* [stay with peace]," was our good-by.

"*Mutikirare* [will you not sleep here]?" the women asked.

"*Tutikirare umuthi, no anga muthenya ungi,*" replied Wambui, which meant, "We will not sleep here tonight, but perhaps we may some other night."

This, I learned, was a formal, polite way to take leave of a Kikuyu village.

Many other afternoons and evenings were spent in the villages seeking to acquire the strange words of the Kikuyu. Eventually the day dawned when I was expected to give a message at the Sunday morning chapel service. The theme of the message had been carefully prepared, but the medium through which it was to be expressed had many missing links. After the opening hymns and a prayer offered by one of the Christian boys, I arose to try out my Kikuyu.

Johana, a pupil-teacher, sat on the front seat, all interest and attention. The Scripture lesson was read from Mark, the only portion of the Bible then translated into the Kikuyu language. The opening sentence of the message was broken and hesitating, and then Kikuyu verbs with their prefixes, infixes, and suffixes failed me as I tried to form the second sentence. Johana rolled his eyes from right to left and then heavenward in a desperate effort to determine what verb the *Bibi* was aiming to use.

"Ni-ci-a-ndi-ke-two," he called out at last in triumph.

"Ni-ci-a-ndi-ke-two," I repeated with a grateful smile. Then together Johana and I finished my first short message to the Kikuyu people, while the small, amused congregation bore with us patiently.

How small many times are the beginnings of great things to follow! Johana and I were destined to go together to many of the bypaths, villages, and conference centers of Kikuyuland during the years to come and to speak together with the Kikuyu people about the things of God.

Chapter 3

SUNSHINE AND SHADOW ON A SCHOOL

THE BATTLE WITH KIKUYU SYNTAX was interrupted suddenly by a call to attend a sick fellow missionary in Ukambaland. Kihoga, who had remained at Matara to become my personal boy, accompanied me on the trip, a particularly adventuresome one, part of which was made on the back of my newly acquired mule, Ndeithia, whose name means "help me."

"*Tiitheru* [of a truth], we have been away a long time," remarked Kihoga when, for the second time since my recent arrival in Kenya, we began to climb the steep path back of Kijabe mission station on the final lap of our journey home after an absence of about six weeks.

Dark clouds began to gather as we reached the plateau, where we lost the path to Matara and spent several hours trying to find it again, and the first large drops of a steady downpour fell when we entered the bamboo forest. We were drenched to the skin and far from Matara when darkness overtook us. There was nothing to do but commit ourselves to the Lord, give the mule the bit, and trust her God-given ingenuity and intuition, of which she had plenty, to take us safely through the night to our destination.

At eleven o'clock Ndeithia stopped near the McKenricks' house. I dismounted and staggered toward the door, too stiff and sore to stand erect. There was a stir within in response to my rap. A light appeared, and in a few minutes the bedraggled traveler was welcomed, warmed, and fed. Tin boxes, small trunks, traveling cases, and safari bags bulging with blankets were scattered about the house. The McKenricks—father, mother, and three children—were packed to leave for furlough the next morning at five.

"I have returned home to study Kikuyu—now what will I do for a language teacher?" I asked as I sipped a cup of hot tea.

"I have told the boys to help you. Johana is a very good teacher," *Bwana* McKenrick reassured me.

In the first gray light of the next dawn, we two remaining missionaries, with a small group of African boys and girls, waved the McKenricks a fond farewell and watched their safari slowly climb the Karimeno River hill and disappear in the forest. Then the *Bibi* McKinstry and I returned to the mission house and sat down in the midst of the confusion to collect our thoughts.

"Here we are," said the senior missionary, "two women, three primitive African teachers just emerging from paganism, fourteen African refugee girls and orphan children left to carry on alone in the bushes."

"What assistance I can, I will give," I offered dismally, "but I know practically nothing about the language or the people."

"Let us take stock," returned the *Bibi* McKinstry, picking up a pad and pencil from a nearby table. "We have the morning school which consists of the girls and children living here in the girls' home and a few boys from the villages who are struggling to read and write the syllables of their language. We have the pupil-teachers—Johana, Zaccheus, and Paul—to help us. You will find it helpful in your study of the language to oversee the morning school."

I gasped at the thought of taking charge of a school, the teaching medium of which was so unfamiliar to me, but my companion continued.

"Afternoon school carries forward a few who have learned to read and gives advanced instruction to the pupil-teachers. I will take charge of the afternoon sessions. We will have to take the Sunday services. Some of the local village people come to these. It will be a good plan for us to alternate in taking the Sunday services. I will take the coming Sunday. You prepare a message for the following Sunday."

"Oh, but I do not know the language sufficiently well to be able to deliver a message," I protested, astonished at such a suggestion.

"To use the vocabulary and knowledge you have gained is the best way to retain it and acquire confidence in the use of it."

This is what led to the giving of that first feeble attempt at a message in the crude chapel, when Johana valiantly rose to my help.

"You will be free in the afternoons to go to the villages to familiarize yourself with the language," *Bibi* McKinstry went on.

The building in which the school assembled was built of slabs sawed by hand. The roof was of corrugated iron, the floor of earth. Slabs supported by short poles driven into the earth in rows with an aisle between served as desks for school and pews for church. During school hours the cardboard squares of syllables were spread out on the seats, and classes gathered in groups around them. With a long pointer, which often was converted into a rod to be used over the head of a dull pupil, the pupil-teacher indicated the syllables to be read. A crude table at which I presided during the morning school stood on the rough platform. A wobbly chair, a homemade blackboard, and an improvised stove completed the furnishings of the school.

The handful of pupils who straggled into the building when the steel rail, which marked the passing of the hours, was struck were a motley lot. There was Giciru, a quiet man of about thirty-five who carried the supply of water for the mission house on his head in a kerosene tin from the spring at the foot of a long hill. There were the houseboy and the cook, the mule boy and the garden boy, a cast-off woman with a baby on her back, a few girls and children who had been sent to Matara from another mission station. Outside, some village herdboys who had disobeyed their fathers' orders and had brought their flocks to feed on the grass of the mission station were curious to know what was going on. They peered through the cracks between the slabs and around the doorpost.

"Will you not come in?" I called to them morning after morning. But when I went to the doorway to give them a further invitation, they darted back like children expecting to be struck for being out of place.

"Come in and learn to read," I urged.

"We will be beaten by our fathers," they replied.

"I want to know the affair of school," said one dirty, bright-faced herdboy, "but my father says schools are the foolish affair of the white man and will never help to bring rupees, sheep, and goats to his village to increase the herd."

"We must try to persuade them to come in to learn to read," I said to the pupils, who were always eager to induce the village children to come to school.

"Leave it to us, *Bibi,*" they said. "We will pull them in with our words."

In time the shepherd boys felt the pull of words and came into school to pore over the cards of syllables.

"*Ma-tu, ma-tu, ma-tu,*" they stammered triumphantly when, for the first time, their ears told them the combination of *ma* and *tu* made the Kikuyu word for cloud.

As the revelation of the mysteries of school unfolded to them day by day, they were keenly interested. But, alas for them, word of their interest reached the ears of their fathers. Stern orders were issued to herd the flocks in pastures far removed from the mission station. However, having tasted of the tree of knowledge, they were not to be deterred from learning to read by a matter of mere strong words or the fear of severe beatings. Every morning some of them would turn up keen and eager to master the affair of reading. Each evening they returned to their villages to find that some busybody had relayed the day's doings to their fathers. With courageous determination they braved the fathers' wrath, took their beatings, and returned to school the next morning.

Morning after morning when the lessons in reading, writing, and numbers were finished, the pupils sat on the slab benches, folded their arms, and repeated the words of the Book of God. They listened attentively to the *Bibi* as she explained to them the affair of God. The words the *Bibi* told them were very good words, they said, as they repeated and discussed them while herding their flocks. They believed the words to be true, and among themselves they decided to follow the Good Shepherd, eat of His pastures, and drink of His waters which the *Bibi* said would never fail.

The school grew and flourished. The *Bibi's* heart was cheered.

"These herdboys," she said to herself as she observed their response to the teachings, "will become the future teachers and evangelists to carry the Good News far and wide in their tribe."

Then one long-to-be-remembered morning the ridges and valleys all about Matara were filled with pagan songs and wild excitement. There was much running about from village to village and calling from ridge to ridge. Men, women, and children had been gathering at various points of the district since dawn. Their bodies were decorated with powdered red or white clay in hideous designs which gave them the appearance of being inhuman. They rang bells, blew whistles, horns, and trumpets made of the crooked necks of gourds, and gazelle horns to accompany their singing. The unruly, agitated mob moved toward the mission station by a path which led through it and passed the school. They were bound for the banks of a nearby river where fifteen Kikuyu boys and girls, nearing the age of puberty, were to undergo the final rites which would introduce them to fullfledged membership in their tribe.

The atmosphere of the little school was tense with excitement as the mob approached. The *Bibi* tried to steady the pupils, but it was to no avail. The powers that ruled Kikuyuland had set the stage with an object in view. Deliberately they had planned to march through the mission station when the school was in session. The effect of the well-known, meaningful songs upon the pupils was that of a strong magnet held over steel filings. As the crowd dashed by, they gave a wild cry. The pupils, with the exception of the teachers, leaped to their feet, shrieked a reply to the call from without, pushed their way through the doorway with mob violence, and were lost in the crowd. Away went the *Bibi's* future evangelists and teachers at one stroke. Dark clouds of discouragement and disappointment lowered and enveloped the morning school at Matara. Would these boys ever return to school again? This was the burning question which clamored for a reply in my mind as I slowly recovered from the first shock of the disaster.

The members of the school who lived and worked on the mission station were in their places when school was resumed again the next morning, but the promising little herdboys were missing. For the time being, the affairs of darkness had more attraction for them than the affairs of light. At the end of the month, however, when the excitement of the celebrations had subsided, several of the herdboys returned to school.

Chapter 4

A GIRL'S DECISION

A Kikuyu girl sat on a fallen tree in a forest in the midst of Kikuyuland. Her garment of dressed goatskin rubbed with a mixture of castor oil and red clay was as soft as satin. Draped under her left arm, caught up on the right shoulder, and tied into position with two narrow leather strings that were fastened to the garment by rosettes of goatskin, it fell in shining, clinging, graceful folds about her well-formed body. Her head was shaved except for a five-inch circle on the top. The stiff kinks of hair were allowed to grow within the circle but were clipped short according to the custom of Kikuyu girls. A wide bandeau made of small chains and beads covered her forehead and was tied into place at the back by leather strings.

Three small polished bamboo sections had been inserted in the large holes in the cartilages of the girl's ears, which it is customary to pierce early in life. The lobe of her ear had been pierced and stretched to surround a polished ring of wood three inches in diameter. Five long strands of blue and white beads hung from her neck. Brass wire wound around and fitted to her wrist by a native blacksmith formed a bracelet fully five inches wide. Another bracelet of the same material was worn above the bend of her elbow and another one, of beads, above that. Brass bracelets like those on her arms were fitted to her legs just below the knees and at the ankle. Her entire body, including the round patch of hair, was done up in a cosmetic preparation of castor oil and red clay. Her skin was soft and velvety, made so by frequent applications of the castor-oil mixture.

The girl had been sent to the forest to cut a load of firewood which would weigh about 150 pounds and which she was expected to carry in a neat load on her back to her mother's hut. Just now she was weaving industriously on a bag of string as she sat on the log, busy with her own thoughts. She told herself that she would weave five rounds on her bag before beginning to cut the wood. In the meantime, perhaps her thoughts would tell her how to escape the troubles she faced in the village.

"I will never willingly go to the village of old Njoroge to become his wife; I want to be bought by a young warrior," she said defiantly aloud. "*Baba* [father] has received and eaten, without my consent, many of my dowry sheep brought to our village by old Njoroge. He has drunk his beer, too. My father will know one day when I fail to return to his village that he cannot force his daughter to marry an old man she does not wish to marry. It is true that I may be seized any day on my way to or from the garden; or even from here I may be carried away by force to the village of Njoroge where I shall be compelled to enter into the marriage rites. *Tiitheru* [of a truth], if I am to escape, I must do it quickly. Two days from now, if I have good luck, I will go to the mission at Matara. Could I not learn to read the words of the Book of God and to walk in the path of God which the mission boys tell us of when they speak to us at the market places? The paths in a Kikuyu village all lead to trouble and sorrow. There is no path of escape, no one to help a Kikuyu girl. I will leave the paths of the Agikuyu to take the path of God."

Her decision made, Keige threw aside her weaving, picked up her crude ax, and began to cut the log on which she had been sitting into three-foot lengths. These she split, piled up to make a load, tied with a strap, and carried home to her mother's hut.

"A girl has arrived from a village near the ridge where Johana's father lives," announced Wambui two days later as she walked into the *Bibi's* room. "She says Johana has preached to them about believing the affair of God, and now she is pulled by a desire to know more about the affair. She wants to live here with us. I have told her if she stays here, she will be asked to remove all her Kikuyu ornaments and garments and to wash the oil and clay from her body. She says she will not refuse to do this if she is given some muslin to wear after she has bathed."

Wambui escorted Keige to the door of the mission house a few hours later to greet the *Bibi.* She was a changed girl on the outside; the change on the inside, a more delicate operation, remained to be accomplished. Great was the rejoicing on the mission station among the boys and girls over one more Kikuyu girl who had heard and heeded the call to walk in the path of God.

News travels fast in Kikuyuland, and word about Keige's whereabouts was passed along until it reached her father's village.

"Who will return to Njoroge the sheep that have gone into my stomach? Not I," raged the father of Keige in great anger at her mother. "How is it that I was deceived into buying an unprofitable woman? What curse rests upon you that you should have borne me a daughter who has left the paths of her father to follow in the ways of the *muthungu* [the white man]? We will leave for Matara tomorrow morning when the birds begin to twitter in the bushes. If you fail to persuade Keige to return with us, you will be beaten and cast to the bushes for the hyenas to feed upon."

"Come to the girls' house and speak to the mother and father of Keige," called Wambui at the open door of the room where I was working at my desk. "They have come to give her cooked food into which they have put medicine. They will drop charms and medicine about the girls' house, too. They think it will break the spell they believe has been cast upon Keige and that she will return home with them."

I went to the girls' quarters to find the Kikuyu elder and his wife seated on a grassy bank pleading with their daughter to return to their village. The palaver lasted for hours. To all of their pleadings and threats Keige made one firm reply.

"I cannot go back to your village. I am here to learn to read the Book of God and to walk in the path of God. The affairs of Kikuyuland prevent a girl from walking in the path of God."

The old man held himself well in hand. Only his gleaming eyes and the deepening tones of his voice revealed what he felt. Now and again the mother jumped to her feet and brandished her garden knife with shrill cries of anger.

"I have no daughter! I have no daughter!" she cried after she had listened to Keige's final reply. "I will return to our village to tie a strap around my neck. I will tie the other end to a high limb of a forest tree and jump."

She shrieked as she uttered the last words and threw earth over her head. Then she turned and staggered down the path. Now it was the father's turn.

"You refuse me, your father?" he demanded.

"I refuse to return to your village," replied the girl.

"Then I refuse you forever and forever," said the old man, and lifting his staff, he bent it under his foot until it snapped in two.

As the staff cracked and broke, Keige blanched and shrank, but she watched her father steadfastly. Rising to his feet and swinging the broken staff around his head, he began to curse her. His eyes blazed, his voice trembled.

"My body is not your body! My blood is not your blood! My flesh is not your flesh! You are not mine. You are dead! We are parted forever and ever!"

With these words he threw the broken staff with a force

which sent it whistling through the treetops, and having done his worst, he turned his back upon Keige and beckoned his wife to follow him down the path. Instead of doing so, Keige's mother turned upon her daughter with the venom of a reptile about to strike its last blow.

"Keige!" she shrieked. "Where is your home? You have no home. My hut is not your hut. My garden is not your garden. My fire is not your fire. My cookpot is not your cookpot. You have no father! You have no mother! You have no brother! I did not give birth to you. I did not rear you. You have no home, none, none!"

Keige arose silently and disappeared into the girls' house. She emerged with her Kikuyu ornaments wrapped up in her goatskin garments. Solemnly she handed the bundle to her mother in token of her decision to make a complete break with her old life and its customs.

"These," said the father, pointing to the bundle, "will be thrown on a *mbirira* [grave]. To us you are dead. A man never receives the dowry sheep of a dead daughter."

By this remark he meant his daughter to understand that she never could be married. It was intended to be the greatest shame and blow which could be dealt her.

The father reached for his spear which he had thrust into the ground beside him. The mother put Keige's Kikuyu outfit into her string bag and slung it on her back. Turning down the broad path that led away from the mission station, they disappeared over the ridge in the direction of their distant Kikuyu village.

" 'Think not that I am come to send peace on earth: I came not to send peace, but a sword. For I am come to set a man at variance against his father, and the daughter against her mother. . . . And a man's foes shall be they of his own household,' " I murmured as I left Keige after a few comforting words and went to take up the next item on the day's program.

" 'Get thee out of thy country, and from thy kindred, and from thy father's house, unto the land that I will show thee . . . and I will bless thee, and thou shalt be a blessing.' "

So Keige came out from among them, from her kindred, from her father's village, from her mother's hut, to walk in the path that God had marked out for her.

God speaks to us. He will speak in the silence of any waiting spirit, impressing His will and saying, "Get thee out." The perpetual summons of God to men and women, generation after generation, has been: "Come out from among them, and be ye separate, saith the Lord, and touch not the unclean thing; and I will receive you."

Does not the voice that spoke to Abraham, to Elijah, to Peter, to Luther, to Keige, speak to you? Let nothing hinder your obedience; strike your tent and follow where the God of glory beckons; and in that word "Come," understand that He is moving on in front. If you would have His companionship, you must follow.

Chapter 5

SHOWERS OF BLESSING

It was Wednesday evening. Six o'clock, the time "when the goats go into the huts," according to the Kikuyu way of reckoning, had passed into the time "when it grows shadowy, and there is both light and darkness," 6:30. The time, "when stumps look like people, and things look as if they were hyenas, when one is afraid to walk alone," 6:30 to 7:30, was arriving.

The clear, silvery peals of the mission bell from its high platform near the chapel had sounded out through the cool evening air across the valleys and ridges of Matara. To the multitudes living in the villages, as they hustled about to build the fires, put on the cooking pots, and divide the goats to drive them into the various huts, the peals of the bell had no meaning. To the boys and girls living on the mission station, it was a call to go to the chapel to praise, to pray, and to talk about the ways of God.

Down the wide path leading from the girls' and children's quarters just behind the white teachers' house came the pad of bare brown feet. Some of the girls were singing, others were chattering, but all seemed very happy. The boys emerged from their huts near the main path below the chapel. They were more dignified, but alert with interest as the merry girls marched past them and took their places on the front slab seats. The first hymn was announced by the *Bibi* in charge. The parable of the sower was read and explained. The time of prayer one for the other and for the people living in the surrounding villages was over. Now these who were the result of the first seed-sowing in Kikuyuland were to have a time of praise and thanksgiving and to tell how the Lord had led them. Paul was the first to speak.

"When I was a small boy herding my father's sheep and goats," said he, "the first white people of God to pass through our district stopped to tell us about the Son of God. The white people went away, but their words were left behind to work in my heart. I heard that these white people had built a village on Matara Ridge. One day I came here to this school, a foolish little shepherd boy with no wisdom. Here I have learned to write and to read the words of the Book of God. I offer praise before you all to the Good Shepherd who found me herding my father's sheep. He called me to follow Him, and He has been with me all the days."

Giciru the water carrier arose as Paul sat down. He rarely smiled, and there were times when he seemed to be lost in his thoughts. He would stand by a tree, his water tin beside him, and look away over the ridges into space. Some said he was trying to think his way out of his troubles; others said he was sad because no girl in Kikuyuland would consent to her father receiving Giciru's sheep as her dowry. He was keen in school and one of the most attentive listeners when the words of God were being read and explained. Now, as he stood there in the dim light and began to speak, every ear was open to hear what he had to say.

"I have much sorrow and carry heavy loads like stones in my heart," he began. "I am a person with a hot temper. It lives within my breast like a sleeping leopard. When it is roused within me, it causes me to do and say things I otherwise would not do and say. I am a castaway, but I hear you read from the

Book of God that *Jesu* said: 'Him that cometh unto me I will in no wise cast out.' I want to come to *Jesu* now. If He can help me, may He help me; I cannot help myself."

Everyone knew the tragic circumstances which were responsible for the stones in Giciru's heart. He had plunged a garden knife into the abdomen of his father's wife during a dispute over a garden boundary five years before. As he sat down, someone began to sing:

> I hear Thy welcome voice,
>   That calls me, Lord, to Thee
> For cleansing in Thy precious blood
>   That flowed on Calvary.
>
> I am coming, Lord!
>   Coming now to Thee!
> Wash me, cleanse me in the blood
>   That flowed on Calvary.

In that evening hour, Giciru, the murderer, found Jesus. The burden of his heart rolled away as he received cleansing through the blood of the Lamb of God. Zaccheus looked on intently and then got slowly to his feet. He was one of the baptized boys left at Matara by *Bwana* McKenrick to help in the work.

"Many thoughts have fought a war in my heart since *Bwana* Makena went home to America," he confessed. "I came here to learn to read when Matara station was first opened. I have learned not only to read and write and reckon with numbers, but I have learned many other things which we never hear about in Kikuyu villages. I know I have been adopted and made a son of God. But after the *Bwana* went away and we were left to help the *Bibis, Cetani* tempted me. He put into my heart the thought of leaving Matara to go to Nairobi to seek for work which would give me a higher wage than I receive here. He suggested to me that I was wasting my days at Matara. When I came to this meeting, I was almost deciding to go to Nairobi at the end of this month. Here I have listened to the words of Giciru. I see that the Spirit of God is working in the hearts of the people in this place, and has He not worked in my heart, too? He has been saying to me this evening:

" 'Remain at Matara to help these *Bibis* who have come to our bushes to teach us of the One who has power to remove stones from hearts which have been weighted down like that of Giciru.' "

"*Tiitheru* [of a truth]," exclaimed Johana, jumping up as Zaccheus sat down. "I feel that the Spirit of God is working in our midst. I remember the time when I was a small boy herding my father's sheep and goats. The first white man I ever saw came to our village. The women and children very, very frightened. They ran to their villages and cried:

" 'Kill a sheep and sacrifice it, or we die. We looked upon a face like the face of God. It is white!'

"The man had some Kikuyu porters with him to carry his tent and food. He was *Bwana* Sywulka, the man of God who first opened Matara station. He spoke Kikuyu and called us together to tell us about the love of the Son of God. It was the first time we had heard of Him. The *Bwana's* words were to me like the taste of honey. After a few days he left our ridge to camp on another ridge and told the people there the good affair he had told us. I left my father's herd with another herdboy while I went to the ridge where the tent was pitched to hear more of the white man's words about the Son of his God. My father came for me. He was very angry. He gave me a beating and forbade me to listen to the affair of the white man. But the words I had heard were not to be forgotten.

"One day I, too, left the goats to follow some Kikuyu travelers who said they were going to Matara where the man of God lived. Though my father came for me many times and was very angry when I refused to return with him, in time he became discouraged and disinherited me. God has helped me to learn to read the words spoken by *Jesu* which are written in the Book of *Mariko.* His words burn like a fire in my heart. Now I study Swahili[1] very much because I want to read all of the words of God which have been printed in a Book.

"I have a great desire," continued Johana, "to go over all of the ridges of Kikuyuland to explain to all the small herdboys the good affair of salvation from the wages of sin, just as *Bwana* Sywulka explained it to us that day when he first came to our ridge. Pray for me that I may become wise in the ways of teaching the affair of God."

The closing hymn was sung in a spirit which made one aware of the presence of the heavenly Dove. Quietly the boys and girls arose and stole away to disappear through the darkness in the direction of their quarters.

"We sow in hope," I whispered to myself as I left the building. " 'In the morning sow thy seed, and in the evening withhold not thy hand; for thou knowest not which shall prosper, either this or that, or whether they both shall be alike good.' Some seed has fallen into good ground. It is God who gives the increase."

[1]The trade language of East Africa, into which the entire Bible was translated at an early date.

Chapter 6

MUHUTHU

"WHERE ARE THE SHEEP?" asked the father of Muhuthu as he staggered into his village from a near-by beer drink.

"I do not know," replied Muhuthu's mother. "He has probbly taken them to the mission to stray into other men's gardens while he wastes his hours on the foolish affairs of the white man."

"What!" roared the father. "Has Muhuthu returned to follow the affair of school?"

"I tell you he reads every morning and leaves the sheep to stray into other men's gardens," repeated his mother. "You will have a large fine to pay for food destroyed unless you find a way to prevent him from reading when he should be herding."

"A-o-u-! A-o-u-!" shrieked Muhuthu's father, giving the war cry and throwing his sword high into the air. "Has the medicine we bought from the witch doctor failed to destroy his desire for the white man's God, or did you not put it into his food?"

"I mashed the medicine into his food and sat in the hut while he ate it. I know it went into his stomach. I tell you the mission people put very strong medicine into the food they give the boys and girls at the mission. It kills the effect of the charms the witch doctor sells to us to give them."

Half an hour later the father of Muhuthu dashed in among

the herdboys as they sat around the table in the schoolroom with the *Bibi,* forming Kikuyu words from syllables printed on the cardboard squares. Seizing Muhuthu by the nape of the neck as a cat pounces upon a rat, he thrust him outside, before the astonished *Bibi* and the school knew what had happened.

"Gather up your bones. Find your sheep and take them to the place you have been told to herd," he ordered the boy after he had thrown him with violence on the hard path. "*Tiitheru* [of a truth], am I the father of a boy who will turn away from the affairs of his father to follow the cursed things of the white man?"

Muhuthu was one of the herdboys who had returned to read three months after the morning on which he had disappeared in the crowd that marched past the school on their way to perform initiation rites at the river. More and stronger charms had been bought from the witch doctor to put into his food and place about his mother's hut to break the spell the white man was believed to have cast upon him. But it was to no avail. Muhuthu returned to school one day to say that he had turned his back upon his father's village.

"I am pulled by the words of God," he told the *Bibi,* "and I have found that the affair of God and the affairs of *Cetani* cannot live together at peace in one heart. I want to walk in the path of God. Will I be given some work to do that I may buy my food and pay the school fees?"

Muhuthu was given the work of sweeping the floors and washing the dishes. As the days and weeks came and passed, this boy of the bush was initiated into a new world with a new outlook. All the new thoughts and ideas came with great force to this receptive heart which had been steeped in animistic beliefs of which fear was the chief characteristic. He, with the youth of his age, had been instructed thoroughly concerning the ramifications, causes, and effects of tribal *thahu* (uncleanness) for months before and during the initiation rites and ceremonies.

They were given a glimmering view of an unseen world peopled with ancestral spirits and a vague god of the Agikuyu who must be propitiated by sacrifices lest evil befall the tribe, the village, the individual and his possessions. Into the heart of Muhuthu, thus prepared to live a life in pagan Kikuyuland, fell the seed that opened a tomb.

The good news of the message from God of salvation by grace through faith in Jesus Christ was driven home to the heart of Muhuthu and others of his class line upon line, precept upon precept, here a little and there a little. It was illustrated from many points of view by stories from Kikuyu life, by the stories from the Old Testament which tell of God's dealings with His children, His definite laws for them, His hatred of sin, His love for them—anything to bring them out of the mists of ignorance and show God to be a Father who loved them and who had devised a plan of salvation to deliver them from all their enemies. The Jewish laws of the Old Testament resembled those of the Agikuyu. They were easily understood and led to the New Testament which tells of Jesus, the only begotten Son and world Redeemer. Bible pictures helped to impress the teachings on their minds. Hymns such as, "Jesus Loves Me," "What a Wonderful Saviour Is Jesus," and "Nothing but the Blood of Jesus" engraved the great truths of the Scriptures upon their memories. But the Holy Spirit worked the miracle of a new creation in their hearts.

One Sunday afternoon Muhuthu and two of his friends from the mission had been telling God's Good News from village to village and to groups here and there along the paths, who were herding their flocks or engaged in the endless, ever-present palavers for which the Agikuyu are noted. They had just left Muhuthu's father's village when two of his pagan cousins with two warrior companions sprang from a clump of bushes, seized Muhuthu, and ran in the direction of the Chania River, made swift and treacherous by the recent rains.

"*Bibi! Bibi!* Johana! Johana!" cried the companions of Muhuthu as they rushed breathlessly up the path in the direction of the mission house. "Muhuthu has been seized and thrown into the Chania River. He will be lost; he is being swept toward the rapids."

They paused now and again to punctuate their statements with the Kikuyu war cry, a signal to all the countryside that danger is near. From their huts or from the midst of roadside conversations sprang the mission boys as if by magic to follow Johana and Muhuthu's companions through the bushes toward the banks of the river. As they dashed along the path, they snatched a rope used to tether the mule. Throwing this to the struggling Muhuthu, now nearing a point where the waters tumble over a rocky ledge to break into foam spray as they strike the basin of stone a hundred feet below, they called to him to lay hold of the rope. They watched for one tense moment with bated breath, and then there arose a cry.

"He has it! He has it! Pull, boys! Pull him to shore!"

The friends of Muhuthu drew him slowly but surely to the bank of the river and stretched him out on the grass, more dead than alive. Prompt methods were used to revive him. Tenderly, he was carried back to his mission hut, where a huge fire was built to warm him, amid great celebrations and rejoicings.

"It is the charms of the white man's God that saved him," said the father of Muhuthu to his mother that evening.

"I felt a Presence with me which lifted me above the strong currents of lashing water and enabled me to grasp and hold the rope firmly," testified Muhuthu at the midweek prayer meeting.

"Did *Jesu* not say, 'Go ye . . . and preach the gospel,' and, 'Lo, I am with you'?" asked Johana of Zaccheus, as they walked to their hut from the meeting after hearing Muhuthu's testimony.

"He did," replied Zaccheus, "and Muhuthu had been preaching the Gospel when he was seized by those ruffians."

Chapter 7

AFFAIRS OF THE BUSH

THE RAINS of the long rainy season were on. This was a time fraught with many dangers in Kikuyuland. Not only were many travelers swept down to be carried over rapids and lost as they attempted to cross the flooded rivers, but the filth of the villages and the excrement lying about in the bushes, together with the decaying juices of dead, unburied bodies, were washed down the hills by the heavy rains to contaminate the water supply of all Kikuyuland. Epidemics of disease broke out during or after the long rains. These the people attributed to the work of departed spirits which had returned to wreak vengeance on their living relatives for injustices done to them during their lives.

Johana was in the lead as several of us were negotiating the slippery path that led to Chief Kahora's village. Suddenly he left the path to go through the bushes and was followed by Wambui and Kihoga. Cautiously they proceeded, peering into clumps of bushes and under low-hanging branches. I stood in the path with Ndeithia, quite at a loss to know what this detour through the bushes was all about. Presently I saw Johana stop.

"I have found him," he called to his companions, who had gone off to search in other directions. "*Bibi,* come."

We all gathered around Johana.

"I heard this morning," he explained, "that Njoroge *wa* Njuguna had been caught by the sickness of dysentery and was taken to the bush last night. Many people on this ridge of Ngabuya and the ridge on the other side of the river are dying of this sickness."

He led us a few yards beyond to the place where Njoroge, the once proud, dignified Kikuyu elder and a member of Kahora's council, lay. He was deserted in the bushes where he had been carried by the men of his village to breathe out his last, unattended and alone. The man was conscious. He opened his eyes when Johana spoke to him. His lips moved, but he was too weak to speak.

"Would the people of his village help us to carry him to Matara?" I asked. "We could make a stretcher of poles and sticks."

"They have finished with Njoroge," said Kihoga. "They will never agree to touch him again. Besides, the witch doctor of Ngabuya will spread an evil report about us if we take him to the mission. Do you know what they will tell the people, *Bibi?*"

I shook my head.

"They will tell the people not to be deceived by the white people when they say they take sick people from the bushes to heal them, for in truth they take from their bodies the liver, heart, and lungs. These are dried, powdered, and sent to their lands to be sold for great sums of money."

"Well," I replied, "the Lord being our Helper, we will send this old man back to his village with his liver, heart, and lungs in working order. Then what will the people say?"

Kihoga, being fleet of foot, was dispatched to the mission for help to carry the sick man, while the rest of us searched the bushes for materials of which to construct a stretcher. Just before sundown, we climbed the mission hill, bringing the patient with us. A makeshift bed was constructed in one corner of the woodshed. There we watched over the patient day and night until the disease was controlled and his strength began to return.

"What are you doing, *Bibi?*"

I turned from the patient's bedside, having helped him to down a cup of broth, to see Nduta *wa* Gathecera standing in the doorway of the woodshed. Behind her stood two wee tots, Wanjiru and Njeri, her two small daughters, and Nyambura with her small son, Wainaina. These were the two wives and the children of Gathecera. They were practically the only people in all the surrounding district who came to us for medicine when they were sick.

"I just stopped on my way to the garden to ask for some medicine for Wanjiru. She has a cold," said Nduta smiling her brightest. "*Kai, Bibi,* the medicines of the white people are stronger than the medicines of the Kikuyu."

"Nduta, you must not forget," said I, "that the God who sent us to Kikuyuland blesses our medicines and efforts when we try to help the sick and dying."

"*Tiitheru* [of a truth], I know that is a fact," she replied. "No medicine could have healed this man brought in from the bush dying unless it had been blessed of God."

Wee Wanjiru solemnly swallowed the medicine for her cough, and the interesting Kikuyu family turned to take the path leading down the ridge to their gardens.

"The wife of Nduati in the village next to ours has a sick baby," said Nduta as she was leaving. "I told her to bring the baby to you, but she fears the witch doctor will hear and curse her."

In the late afternoon of the following day, a woman brought a sick baby to the dispensary. Its fever was high and the breathing was short and rapid. The lungs were consolidating.

"Are you Nduati's wife?" I asked.

She nodded assent.

"Your baby is very sick. He should be given great care and

medicine every half-hour. You have no clock in your village. Will you sleep in our village that we may try to help him overcome this sickness?"

"I am not able," she replied. "Nduati will be very angry and will beat me if I sleep away from our village."

I gave her some medicine and instructions, but I knew that witchcraft methods would be used in the village and the child's life would go out. The following afternoon I walked up the ridge path to find her hut. Nduati's village was small and apparently deserted. I called my *"hodi,"* the Kikuyu equivalent for knocking, at the doors of two huts but got no response.

"Oka [come]," answered a voice faintly from within as I knocked at the third hut.

I stooped to enter the low doorway. It was dark inside. I could see some dying coals of fire in the ashes in a depression in the middle of the dirt floor. The mother of the sick baby was alone.

"Are you with peace?" I asked.

"I am with peace," she replied slowly and sadly.

"Is your baby sleeping?" I ventured to ask.

"He sleeps in the bushes," she said dejectedly.

Did she mean she had been compelled by custom to take him to the bushes to die there and that he was still living, or did she mean he was taking his last, long sleep? I could not tell. I did not feel inclined to question her closely; sorrow was breaking her heart. I rose, left the hut, and followed the direction in which she had pointed. I found the baby under a clump of low-hanging bushes. The wee chest had ceased to rise and fall. A life had escaped from the darkness of Kikuyuland and had gone to fairer worlds beyond. I returned to the village and sat down with the woman beside the dying coals of fire.

"Your child has gone to live with God who sent him to live with you for a short time. He will not return to you, but you may go to live in the land where he is now living," I said.

There was only silence.

"Have you heard of *Jesu,* the Son of God, who once lived on this earth, died, and rose again?"

She shook her head.

I sat and spoke with her until the light grew dim outside her hut, but I could get no response and left with no assurance that she had even a ray of hope. She could not hear, she could not see or feel She was dead, dead in trespasses and sin.

Chapter 8

THE BACK THAT CARRIES THE BABY

THE SUN WAS MOVING close to the line where the forest, stretching away toward Kijabe, meets the skyline. Soon it would dip down behind the tops of the trees. The coolness of the beautiful hour of twilight was quietly taking possession of Kikuyuland.

"Come, let us go for a walk," called Wambui and Keige as they strolled down the path.

"I would like to walk," I replied. "Where are you going?"

"We are going down the path that leads to the east," they said. "Come, walk with us."

The Kikuyu women were returning home to their villages from their gardens down the ridge, long lines of them in single file trudging up the ridge path loaded down to capacity, but chattering and laughing merrily or scolding and storming in "words of strength," depending upon the topic of conversation.

"Why do the people living about Matara cultivate gardens so far away from their villages?" I asked the girls. "These women must get very tired. They left their villages early this morning when the birds began to chirp in the bushes. They have cultivated their gardens all day. Now they are carrying these heavy loads home to their villages over this long path. When they reach home, they will have to bring water from the stream, build the fire, and cook large pots of corn and beans and green bananas to serve their hungry families. Dear me, why do they not cultivate land near their villages?"

"*Bibi,*" laughed Wambui, "it is the affair of the sheep and goats. There is plenty of grass and young shrubs for the flocks to feed upon up near the forest line. The forest and bush have all been cleared away down the ridge. The people cultivate there but keep the land near the forest for their villages and flocks."

"I suppose the flocks are of more value to the men of Kikuyu-land than their women," I replied tartly.

"To the men the flocks are as valuable as the women," said Keige. "They say if they do not possess many slick sheep and goats, they cannot buy women."

We neared the line of women. There were nine of them in the first group. The first woman carried yams and beans in her string bags, which were strapped together and suspended from her forehead by means of a loop in the carrying strap. Astride the bags of food perched her two-year-old baby, who had learned by balancing himself and clinging tightly to the loads to ride his mother home from the gardens. The eight other women in the line were bent double with loads of long sugar canes, loads that must have weighed at least two hundred pounds each. After cultivating all day, they had been ordered to the sugar-cane marshes to carry home the cane their husbands had been cutting during the day. It was to be used the next day to make beer for the men. As they paused to greet us, they placed their hands on their thighs to support their loads and looked up into my face from beneath the juicy, garnet-colored canes.

"I would not carry heavy loads of sugar cane home to my village if I were you," I said, unable to conceal the strong re-sentment which seemed to tie my heart in knots. "Tomorrow you will be compelled to work all day in order to crush the cane to pulp in your mortars. You will place the pulp in jars of water, wring from it the sweet juices, put the long seed pods of one of your trees in it to cause it to ferment, and put it in large gourds in a warm place for two or three days. All that hard work to make your men drunk and quarrelsome! No, I would not do it."

The woman at the head of the line threw back her head and broke forth into a gale of laughter.

"Do you hear what the *Bibi* says?" she called to the women behind her, when she had recovered from her laughing spasm.

"No," they replied, "what does the *Bibi* say?"

"She says she would not carry heavy loads of sugar cane home to her village to make beer for her man."

A chorus of laughter followed.

"What does the *Bibi* say she would do if she was commanded to carry it home?" the women asked.

"What would you do?" the first woman asked with keen interest.

"I would lay the load in the bushes by the side of the path," I replied.

Another chorus of laughter followed.

"But does the *Bibi* know what would happen to her if she did that?" they asked.

"Ha," laughed Wambui, "the woman who did that in Kikuyuland would be beaten to within a few breaths of ending her life."

"Go in peace," said the women, taking a fresh grip on their loads. "We carry our loads to our village. It is time to put the food on to boil. We will be beaten if the food is not done when the men call for it. When we meet again, *Bibi,* tell us some of the other things you would not do after you had been bought with sheep and goats."

The women trudged off up the ridge, while I expressed my feelings at length to the girls as we walked on down the ridge.

"I feel much sorrow in my heart for the women of Kikuyuland. They are just like slaves. Their value is reckoned in terms of sheep and goats, the amount of work they can do, or the number of children they will bear, who in turn will help to increase the sheep and goats of the village herd. When a woman grows old and her strength fails and she is no longer able to carry heavy loads or bear children, she may be abandoned. If they are very old and helpless, I know they are sometimes taken for a long walk through a forest in the midst of which they are left to perish, heartbroken and alone. But more than all, the Kikuyu woman has no comfort of the words of God, no hope beyond her life of hardship and toil. No one has explained to her about a life which may be lived midst the glory and splendor of the Father's kingdom."

"Their eyes are blind to the light which we see and feel," replied Wambui slowly. "We must with great zeal tell them the Good News sent to the earth from Heaven."

"Bibi," said Keige suddenly, " I do not want to be bought by a Mugikuyu who is not a man of God. I say the best way to bring light to the women of Kikuyuland is for girls who begin to know the things of God to marry men who know God. Would they not have children who would hear about the things of God and ways of the people of God even when they are small? If there are many families in Kikuyuland who know and follow the words of *Jesu,* would that not spread the knowledge of God and His ways through the tribe?"

"Ha," laughed Wambui, "you, perhaps, have your eye on one of the mission boys. Which boy are you thinking of sending to your father's village to ask your price in sheep and goats? Did your father not tell you that you are dead, and that a dead girl is never bought?"

"I hear them read from the Book of God that all things are possible with God," replied Keige stoutly, "and I believe God is able to help me in all of my affairs."

"Tell us the name of the boy to whom you believe God will give favor when you send him to talk with your angry father," urged Wambui, winking at me on the sly.

But Keige was silent and carefully guarded the secret of her heart.

"I believe Keige has mentioned one of the best ways to bring the light of the knowledge of God to the Kikuyu tribe," said I. "No one can measure the influence and power of a well-ordered Christian home to spread the light of the Gospel of Christ and to stir within the hearts of those who see its fruits a desire to know the secret of its joys and blessings."

Chapter 9

A POTENTIAL CHRISTIAN MOTHER

NEARLY A HALF-HOUR had passed since the 1:30 bell had rung for the girls to get their cultivating knives and go to the gardens. Yet I heard animated conversations still going on in the cookhouse and went to see why the girls were there.

"What!" I exclaimed, opening the door and looking in. "Two o'clock, and you girls are still roasting potatoes!"

"Oh, *Bibi,*" they explained, "it is because of the affair of this stranger girl. She has left her father's village because of much trouble. We met her on the path and told her to come to our house and we would bake some potatoes for her. She has had no food today. She does not know where she is going. We have told her to stay with us and you will teach her about the good affair of the love of God."

Wanjiru *wa* Cege sat in their midst arrayed in all the finery of Kikuyu ornaments, goatskin garments, and castor-oil cosmetics.

"Will you stay and live with us?" I asked her.

The life she saw about her was all new and strange. She was shy and did not seem particularly interested in staying. It was not our practice to urge girls to come to live at the mission.

Pointing out to them what such a step would mean, we left them to make their own decisions. When I went to say good night to the girls in the evening, Wanjiru was still there. She went to school with them in the morning and looked on as they learned to read their syllables on the cardboard squares. Every day for a week, she went with the girls as they carried out their daily schedule.

"*Bibi,*" called Keige on Saturday morning as the girls passed my door on their way to the river to do their weekly wash, "give us some soap and a cloth for Wanjiru. She wants us to remove her ornaments. Come to the river, *Bibi.* If her people should come for her and a war were to follow, you would be there to help us."

In many ways we did not like the idea of Kikuyu girls exchanging their native garb for one which had been introduced to their land by the white man. It would have pleased us if we could have taught them to abhor the idea of imitating the white man in his ways and habits of life. To have pointed out to them a Christian way of life which was distinctly African, rather than try to fit to them the cumbersome, complicated, and in many ways mistaken customs of the white man's Christianity, would have been ideal. The skin garments, however, had to go for hygienic reasons. The attractive bead ornaments, chains, and copper wire represented evil customs and could not be disassociated in the Kikuyu mind from the practices which they represented. To wear a Kikuyu outfit while professing to live the Christian life was hypocrisy to the pagan mind.

I sat on the bank of the river and watched the girls remove Wanjiru's Kikuyu garb. She stepped into the river and covered her head and body with a thick lather of soap which dissolved the castor-oil mixture and revealed a clear, velvety, light brown skin. As the last trace of the marks of Kikuyu village life disappeared, her face took on a grayish pallor which in the African denotes a deep emotion, and I realized that I was looking upon a scene which to her was like a sacrament. The removal of all her ornaments meant a complete break with her old life and with all they represented in Kikuyu practice. Now she would not be allowed to sleep in her father's village should she return. Her very presence there without her Kikuyu badges would bring uncleanness to the village and all of its occupants. Only the sacrifice of a sheep and a cleansing by blood could restore her to her former position in Kikuyu life.

Wanjiru stepped out of the water surrounded by the girls, who draped and securely fastened a muslin loin cloth around her waist. Two yards of the muslin were draped around her shoulders and under her left arm, and the corners were tied on her right shoulder. In comparison with the beautiful Kikuyu girl who sat in the cookhouse the first time I saw her, she looked like a Cinderella prepared to go to the chimney corner after the ball garments had vanished.

Wanjiru's absence from her father's village had caused a great commotion. Tracers were sent to be on the alert for reports of girls who were known to be gadding about Kikuyuland to avoid affairs in their villages. Hearing that a girl at Matara station had lately taken off her Kikuyu clothes, a disguised tracer loitered near the path to watch the girls as they went about their daily tasks. Spying Wanjiru in their midst, he sped off to her faraway village to report.

Her father, a crafty Kikuyu elder, had lived on a coffee plantation and was well versed in the ways of the white man. He did not propose to tire his legs in making a trip to the mission station. He went direct to a Government post and accused the mission people of stealing his daughter. Having had a debt which he knew he would be forced to pay one day, he had hidden his sheep by twos and threes in the flocks of his widely scattered friends where they would increase and enrich him unbeknown to his creditor. Pressed for a payment on his debt, he had sold

Wanjiru to pay off a part of the debt when she was two years old.

Under these circumstances, children in Kikuyuland are allowed to remain with their mothers until they reach a marriageable age. Wanjiru's mother had explained to her now and again during her young life that she was the property of a certain old man, her father's creditor, but like all Kikuyu girls, she loved the young warriors and wished to marry a certain young favorite. Seeing the usual ceremonies going on in her clan which preceded the time when a buyer would be given permission to take possession of his property, Wanjiru knew her hour was near and had fled in desperation from her father's village. Two days later she had found herself sitting in the girls' cookhouse, undecided as to whether she would remain or push on into Kikuyuland, she knew not where.

"A Government messenger has arrived," announced Kihoga, handing me a letter that bore a seal which read, "On His Majesty's Service."

The letter informed me that Matara mission station was accused of harboring the daughter of one Wanjiru *wa* Cege. An order was hereby given for the girl to come to Kiambu Government Post with the bearer of the letter to appear before the District Commissioner and her father to explain why she had left her father's village.

Dismay filled the hearts of all at Matara as the news spread from group to group. What possible chance did Wanjiru, a timid Kikuyu girl, have of getting a sympathetic or understanding hearing? Under the circumstances, she would be too frightened even to state her case. It was decided that Johana and Kihoga would go with her to see if they could be of any assistance in helping her to present her side of the case and that of the mission.

Two days later the boys returned to Matara with a letter from the District Commissioner. It informed us that, as the father of Wanjiru was her legal guardian, he, as District Commissioner, had ordered the girl to return to her father's village. Expressions of sorrow and sympathy were made by her mission friends when the news reached them. One source of help, however, was still open to them. They appealed to the Father in Heaven and trusted the methods of that One who counts the sparrows and numbers the hairs of His children's heads to watch over and deliver His helpless child.

A month passed, and no word was heard of Wanjiru. Then one day when the girls were cultivating their gardens along the main path which leads to the mission station from a travelers' path stretching through Kikuyu country from east to west, a cry suddenly arose from the garden which sent all mission groups running to discover the cause.

"Wanjiru! Wanjiru!" cried the girls as they rushed to the path to fall on the neck of their lost companion. "How did you escape? What power has delivered you from the power of Kikuyuland?"

"What power has delivered her, do you ask?" called Johana as he ran down the path in the direction of the glad greetings. "Have you not been praying?"

"Who cooked your supper last night?" asked Wambui around the fire in the cookhouse that evening as she dished up a generous plate of food and handed it to Wanjiru.

"Last night," replied Wanjiru quietly, "I slept in a tree. There are no cooks in trees."

"What!" cried the girls. "Slept in a tree? What kind of bad luck sent you to a tree to spend the night?"

"I heard the men from the village of the old man who owns me talking in my father's hut. They were coming today to take me by force. In the early evening after they left, I took my mother's large water gourd and went to the river to get water, but I was afraid I might be seized that evening, so I left the gourd at the river and took a path leading toward Matara. The night caught me. When the hyenas began to howl on the ridges, I was frightened and climbed a tree. There was no moon. I was cold. As I sat on the limb, I prayed to God to keep me from dozing and losing my balance and falling to the ground."

"*Kai,* what will we do about Wanjiru?" I asked Kihoga in the morning. "If her father reports to the District Commissioner that she is being sheltered again at Matara mission, he may become very angry and close this mission station."

"I do not know what can be done," replied Kihoga. "We cannot turn her out and tell her to return to her father."

"It might be a good plan to report the situation to the District Commissioner. Will you and Johana make another trip to Kiambu Government Post to deliver a letter?" I asked.

"Write the letter," said Kihoga.

The next morning before daybreak, the two boys left Matara with the letter.

> Dear Sir:
>
> We wish to report the fact that Wanjiru *wa* Cege has returned to Matara mission. We are providing her with food and shelter. What is your command in the matter?

Back came the reply:

> I will call the father and give you instructions regarding Wanjiru *wa* Cege in due time.

"Let us pray for Wanjiru," said Johana when the boys and girls had gathered for their Wednesday evening prayer and praise hour. "Let us not be frightened at circumstances. Do we not read in the Book of Hebrews that by faith in past times the people of God have won many victories?"

Ten days later a tribal retainer walked up the broad path leading to Matara station. He carried a letter in the split end of a stick. The split parts were pressed together over the edge of the letter and tied securely with a string made of the soft inner bark of an African bush.

"Now we will be told to send Wanjiru back to Kiambu," said Kihoga as he handed me the stick and the letter.

> I have called the father of Wanjiru and have told him that I took the trouble to order his daughter to be returned to him. If he is unable to command her to stay in his village, there is nothing further I can do about the matter.

If another example could be added to the eleventh chapter of Hebrews, it would read something like this: "By faith Wanjiru *wa* Cege was delivered from the snare of the fowler."

Chapter 10

THE *NDUGU* GIFT

THE DARKNESS OF THE NIGHT was beginning to turn gray. Sunday morning was dawning. Kihoga came out of his hut, yawned, stretched, and went to the stable to get Ndeithia. Karunge cooked the porridge for an early breakfast, and I prepared to go with Paul and Johana to Kahora's village for our weekly Sunday service. When we had crossed the Chania River, climbed Ngabuya Ridge, and reached the junction of the village and ridge paths, we met Kahora. He was dressed in his birthday suit, which glistened with a coat of castor oil and soft red clay. His arms and his legs below the knees were bedecked with brass and bead ornaments. A leather shield suspended by a leather string was tied to a belt at the back of his waistline. An elaborate headgear of irridescent, shiny feathers gave him a gala appearance.

"Are you with peace, and where are you going?" he inquired, extending his hand cordially to give me the usual Kikuyu greeting.

"And you? Are you with peace?" we asked.

"I am with peace, and I am on my way to the *muthunguci.*"

"*Muthunguci!*" I exclaimed in surprise. "I heard the *muthunguci* had been banned by Government."

He winced when he heard that I had learned of the Government order. Then he shrugged his shoulders.

"The people have all gone," he said. "They cannot dance the *muthunguci* without their chief."

"But today is the Lord's Day," I replied. "We have come to teach you about Him and His affair. Did you not tell me that if we would come to your village on the day of worshiping Him, you would gather your people together and listen to the words God has spoken to you?"

"I will come another day, *Bibi,*" he promised. "Go to my village, call together the women and children who have been left to keep the village. Teach them all of the good words."

"But, Kahora," I warned him, "another day may never come for you. Besides, if a Government spy should see you today, you would much rather have him find you in your village listening to the words of God, would you not?"

"Your words prick me," admitted Kahora, "but I have promised to be at the dancing ground."

So saying, he waved me toward his village and vanished down the ridge path. The *muthunguci* is danced for about six months once only in each generation. It is a time when the old men and women make an attempt to renew their youth. They borrow the feather headgears, the brass and bead ornaments of the young warriors and girls. Out on the Kikuyu dancing grounds where they danced as young men and women, they endeavor to rejuvenate themselves and enjoy the experience that they enjoyed when life was young and full of vigor. It is a great time for all Kikuyuland. Life practically stands still while they all turn out to see the spectacle. For a time the Government officers did not understand why the chiefs were not executing orders sent out to them from headquarters at Fort Hall. When they discovered the *muthunguci* to be the cause, they sent out an order forbidding the chiefs to allow it to be danced in their districts. Heavy fines were threatened if orders were disobeyed.

"If the Government spies find Kahora dancing the *muthunguci* with his people today, you will hear of a big affair," remarked Paul as we journeyed homeward after a meeting with the few women and children who had been left in the village.

"He will get caught in a trap one of these days, and perhaps he will repent," added Johana.

"Did I not hear that the people are dancing the *muthunguci* over in the district of the father of Keige?" Kihoga questioned.

"Ask Johana," laughed Paul. "He has been there recently. *E-e,* Johana, did the old man receive you when you went to ask the price of Keige in sheep, goats, and rupees?"

"Can a young man speak to an old man about his daughter unless he possesses a herd of many sheep and goats?" counter-questioned Johana, shrugging his shoulders as he evaded giving an answer to Paul's question.

Quietly I listened to the conversation and recalled the time when Wambui had accused Keige of having her eye on one of the mission boys. She had urged her to tell us his name, but Keige had guarded her secret. Now the truth was out. The name of that boy was Johana.

"You are called to come out to greet a chief who says you are his friend," announced Wambui one day soon after this trip to the chief's village.

I went out to find Chief Kahora sitting in the glorious African sunshine surrounded by four of his wives and quantities of Kikuyu food. There were yams, sugar cane, and *ikwa,* a three-to-five-pound tuber which is all starch but very nice when roasted or boiled. The load of one of Kahora's wives consisted of cooked *ndoma,* the large root of the elephant plant, or *dasheen,* used to adorn ornamental gardens in our land, but cultivated by the Kikuyu for food. *Ndoma* is mealy and delicious when properly cooked but rank poison if not steamed for three hours. Another wife carried a string of plantains and a bag of *mukombi,* a grain much prized in Kikuyuland. The white people cook the whole grain and use it as a breakfast food.

Kahora's new bride sat among the other wives with downcast eyes, looking very shy, which is the proper attitude for a Kikuyu bride to assume for at least a month after her marriage. She had carried no load, for Kikuyu brides are not expected to do a stroke of work for a month or more.

"*We muhoro* [are you with peace], *Bibi?*" asked Kahora, rising to greet me with a beaming smile. "I have brought my new wife to greet you with a gift of food."

"You have done a good act in bringing your bride to greet me," I replied. "And where have you bought her?"

"Her father is a squatter on a white man's plantation far upcountry," he informed me gaily.

"So you have bought another wife. I wonder why you want so many wives. It seems to me you are only buying trouble for yourself."

"How so?"

"I have seen that your wives do not live at peace with one another in your village. Should this girl quarrel with the women of your village and run back to her father's village, you would have to weary your legs to journey to that faraway village. Already you have made many a tiresome safari to that upcountry village to try to settle the affairs connected with her dowry price, and you know better than I that affairs connected with her marriage to you have only begun. Her family will make great demands of you as long as she lives in your village. As I see it, the man who wishes to possess many wives is looking for trouble."

"*Bibi,*" said Kahora thoughtfully, "you probably are right, but how will people know that Kahora is a rich chief if they do not see the hillsides about him filled with villages of huts built for his wives?"

"The reasonings of your head tell you one affair, and those of mine tell me another," I answered. "Perhaps the heads of the white man and the black man will always tell each a different story, but in the matter of our hearts, the Son of God came to give us God's thought which is the same regarding all of us, for all have sinned. But whoever hears the words of *Jesu* and believes on Him that sent Him has everlasting life."

"I believe the words of those who have come to tell us the words of God," replied the chief.

"What is the name of this very nice bride who has come to greet me today?" I asked.

"Her name is Njambe, and I paid a great price for her. But, here, receive the food we have brought and know that from now on we are *nduguini.*"

After the guests had been served with tea and plenty of sugar, they bade us to stay with peace and slowly made their way homeward, for Kikuyu brides are allowed to take their time and must not be expected to hurry.

"Bibi," called Kihoga from the dining room, where he was laying the table for supper, "do you know the meaning of *nduguini?"*

"Not exactly," I replied.

"To accept a gift of food which is said to be a *ndugu* gift means that you are bound to befriend the giver if any trouble befalls him, and he will do the same by you. *Ndugu* is a very strong bond in Kikuyuland which lasts through to the end of the lives of the *ndugu.*"

"Dear me," I gasped. "What trap has the wily Kahora led me into by bringing all of this food to me today? Why did you not tell me the meaning of *ndugu* before I allowed him to leave the food? Perhaps I could have persuaded him to accept pay for it."

"No," laughed Kihoga, "he would have accepted no pay for this food. It was *ndugu* from the time the plantains were cut from the tree and the *ikwa* dug from the ground. Later on we shall see what is behind his gift to you today, and then I will advise you what to do."

A week passed after Kahora had deposited his *ndugu* gift on the grass of our Matara home. Then I looked out my bedroom window one morning toward the eastern sky and wondered what events would make up this day's program. There were sure to be unscheduled numbers to be reckoned with, for life never was dull on a station in the midst of Kikuyu tribal life. Leaving my bedroom, I went out on the veranda to fill my lungs with refreshing highland air.

"*Bibi,*" called Wambui a few minutes later when she came into the storehouse to get the girls' supply of food for the day, "whom do you suppose has come from Kikuyuland to live with the girls and learn to know the affair of God?"

"I never could tell you."

"Keige's sister arrived late last night and has slept in the girls' house. *Tiitheru* [of a truth], she has made up her mind to turn her back on the affairs of Kikuyuland to walk in the path of God."

"So the sister of Keige has come," I heard Karunge say to Kihoga after Wambui had disappeared with her basket of food. "*Tiitheru* [of a truth], there is another girl for one of the mission boys to buy. I am surprised at the rate girls are leaving Kikuyuland to walk in the path of God. It will be our good luck if the day ever arrives when all of us can buy a mission girl for a wife instead of having to buy one who knows only the dark ways of the Agikuyu. A man who is married to a heathen girl never can move forward. He may put clothes on her and cause her to look like a Christian, but if her heart is unchanged by the Spirit of God, she is still heathen, and the two cannot walk together in the path of God. What say you, Kihoga? I hear you went to the village of the father of Wanjiru last week. Did you have good luck?"

"His price is very high," answered Kihoga dejectedly. "Where will the sheep to make even the first payment come from?"

"You are the only son of your mother, and you have four sisters who have been bought," pointed out Karunge. "Go to your mother's village and demand some of the sheep that were paid for your sisters. You could go to the men who have bought your sisters. You know that each of them should give you some sheep when you are ready to make a payment on the girl who is to become your wife. Your sister—who is living here with the mission girls—I hear Zaccheus has his eye on her. Will the sheep he pays for her not buy a wife for you?"

"Zaccheus is a mission boy, too, and you know the boys of the mission never have many sheep to pay down on a girl. Wanjiru's father demands a payment of thirty sheep before he will even talk," said Kihoga, still dejected. "A man's troubles begin when he has to think about buying a girl."

When the bell rang for the afternoon school session to begin, four Kikuyu men turned off the travelers' path to take the road leading up to the mission station. Two of them were warriors and looked like messengers from a chief's village.

"Are you with peace?" they asked as I met them on my way to see if all the girls had left for school.

"We have been sent by Kahora," they said. "He has been seized by the soldiers of the Government who are taking him to Fort Hall for trial. He will be imprisoned unless he can raise five hundred rupees. He has sent us to inform all of his *ndugu* of the trouble which has caught him. Kahora has many *ndugu.* If each one will send him a gift, the fine of money will appear. The *ndugu* of a chief never allow him to be imprisoned for lack of the help they can give him."

The warriors made their speech and watched me keenly to see what my reaction would be.

"Why has Kahora been seized by soldiers from the Fort?" I asked.

"We do not know why they took him. He was seized when

we were in the midst of the *muthunguci,"* they said, unaware of the fact that we knew of the prohibition of the dance.

"Tell Kahora," I said, "that I told you to ask him this question: Which is the most valuable help a *ndugu* can give to his friend, to warn him about a thief before he takes his sheep, or to try to help him recover the sheep after they have been stolen?"

"We will ask him," they said and departed.

Chapter 11

THE FIRST VILLAGE SCHOOL

"WE HAVE COME to talk to you about a building for a school," I said to Kahora when we had finished the food he had called upon one of his numerous wives to set before us.

The rule of the British Government was to the effect that permission for a school or preaching center could not be granted without the consent of a landowner and the desire on the part of some of the people living in the district for such a center to be built.

"*Bibi,*" said the chief earnestly, "I want to build a house near my village where my boys may go to learn the affair of reading and writing. To have boys who are able to write messages I wish to send to the Fort would help me very much. It is the stupid women who do not understand. They say they will be unable to prevent the small girls from going to read. Kikuyu women believe only trouble and curses will come to them if girls begin to read. Can you not deal with the women and change their hearts?"

"The best way to change their hearts in the matter," I replied, "is to teach all the girls who wish to come to school the affairs we have come to teach them and thus prove to the women that, instead of the curses they believe will overtake them and their girls, blessing will come to them like showers of rain upon a garden planted with corn and beans. Let us select the site today and decide upon a date to prepare to build."

He looked down at the ground perplexed and troubled. The Agikuyu, by a series of putting off until another day, usually can evade a matter they do not wish to tackle. This *Bibi* was pinning him down to act today. How could he put her off? This I knew was the real problem Kahora was turning over in his mind.

"We shall need boys with *pangas* [long knives]," the *Bibi* said, "to cut down the bush on the site and other boys to level off the plot and dig holes for the posts of the framework. Some men should be sent to the forest to cut posts and poles. We shall need nails and banana bark—oh, and the Government permit. When are you going to Fort Hall?"

"On the day of the second," he replied meekly.

"Will you tell the District Commissioner you are giving a plot of ground for a village school and ask him to give you a building permit?"

"I will ask him," he said.

"What day shall we come to build? Would Saturday not be a good day?" asked Paul, and Johana added enthusiastically:

"We could bring the Matara school people over to help your people."

By this time, if the chief was of a doubtful mind concerning the building of the school, there was nothing to indicate that he feared the women's attitude toward the new institution. He was all out for a school in which his boys would be taught to read and write.

"The permit will be here by the day of the sixth, Saturday, and the people will be here to work," he agreed.

Saturday dawned clear and bright. The Matara boys left early for Ngabuya to break soil for the first village school to be launched in Matara district. They arrived to find Kahora marshaling his forces. One group was directed to go to the forest to cut and bring poles. Another group was instructed to clear the brush off a large plot selected for the building. Still others were sent to a nearby garden to gather banana bark. All worked merrily and enthusiastically. At the close of the day, the framework of the building was up, and the bark was on hand to thatch the sides. On the next Saturday the bark was put into water to make it pliable, each long piece was wrapped over the light poles which had been nailed lengthwise to the sides of the building, and the ends of the bark were pulled to the outside. The inside looked very neat with its row after row of rich brown bark. The outside was shaggy, but when the boys finished a side, they took a sharp knife and trimmed off the ends of the bark to make the rows of thatching straight and even.

The building was to be a school and chapel combination, and the opening was scheduled for the first Sunday of the following month. The men and boys were very pleased with themselves. They were looking forward eagerly to the day when they would begin to read. But there was much whispering going on among the women, who were filled with dark forebodings. However, when the day came for the opening, women and children were seen gathering around the new center.

"Their curiosity has eaten up their opposition," laughed Wambui as our Matara delegation neared Kahora's village.

Johana gave the message of the morning, Paul led the singing, and Zaccheus offered the opening prayer. The singing was a joyful noise unto the Lord as the congregation endeavored to sing Kikuyu words to the old Gospel tunes. Johana spoke the words of God to the people as only he could speak to them from "God so loved the world, that he gave . . ."

"He gave," said Johana, "His love which sent His one and only beloved Son. He gave a way of salvation from darkness, sin, and death. He sent His messengers to explain that way to all the tribes of the earth. The Good News has now reached Ngabuya Ridge. God has put it into the hearts of His people to give you a building where you may gather day by day to hear what God has said to you and to learn how to follow the directions He has sent to you. May you receive His words, His Son, and walk in His way with Him. From this day on you are without excuse."

The service was about to close, but there was one important announcement to be made. Paul would be there to open the school Monday morning.

"Come and learn to read and write when you hear us blow the gazelle's horn from Kahora's village," he said.

"*Ni wega* [that is good]," the congregation replied.

A boy volunteered to go to Matara to carry the hinged-top wooden box of school supplies for Paul when he returned the next morning. The box contained a biscuit tin of cardboard squares with the vowels and Kikuyu syllables. There was a roll of charts containing the first hymns translated into Kikuyu, and a Kikuyu Gospel of Mark. A small blackboard which had been given a fresh coat of black paint completed the equipment.

"I have brought my boys to your school," said Kahora, as he appeared with ten small boys from his village after the gazelle horn had been sounded for the first session of school. "I want you to make them wise in the wisdom of the white man that they may grow to become the wise men of Kahora and thus increase my fame."

"Do not forget," replied Paul with a smile, "that I have come to your ridge to make you wise not only in the wisdom of schools. The best teaching I have to give you and your boys is this: To as many as receive the Son of God, He gives the right to become His sons. Kahora, do you and your sons not wish to be called, in truth, the sons of God?"

"It is a good affair," he assented. "We will listen to all you have to teach us."

Boys from other villages came to the opening session, and a few of the elders came late to pay their respects to the new affair which had been launched in their midst. The children whose names were recorded in the first roll book of Ngabuya village school were typical of all Kikuyu pupils when they first aspire to grasp the affairs of the white man's school. The matter of arriving on time at a given place when a horn is sounded was a new idea. The Agikuyu have no cut and dried program when they open their eyes to the light of a new day morning by morning. Perhaps they will take a journey or cultivate their gardens, but if another impulse stirs them to pursue other things, what difference does it make about the journey and the garden? To leave their villages when the gazelle horn sent its sharp call over the Kikuyu morning air, to arrive at school in time to sit in their places when the morning hymn was announced, were the first lessons Paul tried to teach his pupils.

Education, as we know it, is hard for primitive Africans to understand. It is difficult in the beginning for them to grasp abstract ideas and to learn things from books. Their background has not prepared them to grasp the white man's method of learning. Hundreds of generations without a book or a written word, and suddenly to have their names enrolled in a village school! In that primitive school the way that leads to the village of God, the truth that makes wise unto salvation, would be made clear to all those who would come to hear and then go their ways through the African world. How many of these would be among the multitude redeemed to God by the blood of the Lamb out of every kindred and tongue, people and nation who are to be made a kingdom of priests to reign with Christ upon the earth when God extends His hand to lay aside all earthly authority? These thoughts coursed through my mind as I sat in their midst during the opening session and looked out upon the years to come.

"This has been a great day for all of us who live in this section of Kikuyuland," I said to Paul as we journeyed home. "God is the Harvester and we are the sowers. We have His everlasting promise which has been made to each succeeding generation of sowers, 'My word that goeth forth out of my mouth: it shall not return unto me void, but it shall accomplish that which I please, and it shall prosper in the thing whereunto I sent it.' What a wonderful privilege and opportunity we have now to sow that powerful Word in the hearts of the people living on Ngabuya Ridge, assured that the harvest will be certain! We may never see the results of our sowing, but let us be faithful and tireless in scattering abroad the living words of God."

"We will scatter it," replied the boys thoughtfully as we climbed the last hill which would land us on the ridge of Matara.

Chapter 12

A WEDDING

A TWO-ROOMED HOUSE of poles and banana-bark thatch, with a door and windows, was being built at Matara for a bride and groom. It was the first step in advance of the dark, smoky, cluttered hut toward better and more healthful houses for African homes in that section of the tribe. The boys and girls on the station were much excited at the prospect of a wedding in their midst, for the banns had been published in the church for the wedding of Johana and Keige. The *Bwana* McKenrick had returned from America after his furlough and soon would be back at Matara to marry them.

"*Bwana* McKenrick will come to Matara on Monday. The following Wednesday will be your wedding day," I explained to Johana, who had come to inquire about the latest news from Kijabe concerning the coming great event in his life.

"By that time we will have the house finished," he said, "and the last sheep and gifts required by the father of Keige for the present will have been taken to his village. It is a big affair, *Bibi,* to begin to buy a girl and brings with it a heavy load."

"All worth-while things in this life require effort and sacrifice on our part," I replied. "Think of what it will mean to you through the years to have a Christian wife like Keige to help you and share with you all the program God has planned for your lives together if you will walk with Him. What a great honor and privilege you and Keige are to have in establishing the first Christian Kikuyu home at Matara! The eyes of all will be upon you. Many probably will follow in your steps. How carefully you must walk, asking God to give you strength to follow as He leads day by day that others may not stumble as they follow the path you are cutting through the unknown forest of Christian marriage with all that it means to the young men and women of Kikuyuland and their children!"

"We will try to follow as the Master leads and directs," he said, and his face lit up with the smile for which he was noted.

"I see *Bwana* Makena and his white mule coming down the Karimeno hill," announced Wambui a few days later. "There is another mule, too. *Bibi* Makena is riding it."

The boys and girls of the station were overjoyed as they ran down the path to the Nyakibai River to give vent to their feelings of genuine joy and thanksgiving to God for preserving the lives of their *Bwana* and *Bibi* during their long journeys over the trackless oceans and for returning them to Matara safely. Never in all the world were people given a more truehearted, royal welcome than that given to returning beloved teachers by simple, loyal Africans living beyond the outposts of civilization.

In the days that followed the arrival of the McKenricks, everyone was busy at Matara and everyone's mind was on the wedding.

"We must organize the work which will have to be done in connection with the wedding," we said to the girls as they sat around their cooking pot at noontime. "Tomorrow will be market day. We must choose four girls to go to the Ndonyo market to buy the bananas and food for the wedding feast. Everything in the way of food must be collected and prepared tomorrow. We will have the decorating of the chapel and the cooking of the food to look after the next morning. We will ask Wanjiru and Nduta to take charge of the cooking. They may choose the girls to help them. Nyambura and Wambui may choose girls to help them gather ferns and flowers to decorate the chapel."

Keige sat in the background listening to the chatter. She looked very solemn and serious but had nothing to say. Weddings in Kikuyuland are an affair of weeping and wailing for the bride. Keige was well acquainted with the Kikuyu point of view, but the attitude of white people toward Christian marriage was hard for her and all Kikuyu girls to understand. We had talked with her about the new life and relationships she was about to enter—the responsibilities, privileges, and honors connected with Christian marriage—but it was all new and vague to her. After all, she had not been long in the Christian way and was not far removed from her Kikuyu background.

When the *Bwana* had arrived and learned of the village school at Kahora's and also that Paul had been making payments on Njeri, one of the newer mission girls, he encouraged Paul to finish off his negotiations with the father of Njeri, an irate old heathen man whose village was on our very borders. With the help of the *Bwana,* the Kikuyu elder was brought to terms and gave his consent for Njeri to marry Paul. So, at the last minute, we learned that we were to celebrate a double wedding.

Before the birds had chirped their first notes on the wedding morning, there was a great stir at Matara mission station. The usual schedule was abandoned, a holiday spirit took possession of all as they popped out of bed to prepare for the day's celebrations. The final preparations must be finished by ten o'clock. The weddings were scheduled for 10:30. Wambui and her corps of helpers had scattered about the edge of the forest and in the ravines. They were gathering bushels of trailing asparagus ferns and maiden hair. Small tree ferns, periwinkle, forest begonia, and the pastel flowers of the forest were among the sweet-smelling collection brought to the chapel before the sun peeped over the hills to see what was going on. Wanjiku had taken her group to the bush to cut the extra dry wood needed to cook the wedding feast. Wanjiru and Nduta with their group were paring potatoes, washing rice, cutting up meat, and collecting cooking pots.

"Ask the *Bibi* to give you the large brass kettle she uses to heat her wash water," called Wanjiku to the girls she had sent to borrow all available pots from the surrounding villages.

The *Bibis* flitted about from group to group during the morning hours to see that all was going smoothly and to give a few encouraging words and suggestions now and then. They were keeping tabs on the time, too, to see that all was finished and all the girls had gone to dress for the wedding by ten. The *Bibis* had been elected to dress the brides, who sat huddled over the fire in the girls' house. They had bathed and oiled their skins, but, shy, glum, and solemn, they were far removed from the proverbial smiling bride on her wedding day. They were called to the mission house where they were helped to put on the simple white muslin dresses. The white headcloths were arranged to fall over their shoulders and served as bridal veils.

The chapel bell rang promptly at ten. There was a great scramble around and inside the girls' house to wash hands and faces, get into clean dresses and arrange the head kerchiefs properly for a special occasion. The peals of the 10:30 bell rang out over the ridges. The *Bwana* punctually descended the path and walked briskly in the direction of the chapel. The boys and girls emerged from their quarters to move excitedly in the same direction.

Two tree ferns in all of their forest grandeur stood on guard at the chapel doorway. The interior of the dingy old building, as by the wave of a fairy queen's wand, had been transformed into a bower of fragrant beauty. The *Bwana* stood in his place between two fern trees. In his hand was a book containing the Kikuyu Christian wedding vows. The bridegrooms, with their best man, waited outside the chapel looking anxiously up the path in the direction of the girls' quarters. The congregation waited quietly and expectantly, but the brides did not appear. Up at the *Bibis'* house they sat in solemn silence staring down at the floor. They were arrayed in their bridal attire and ready to move in the direction of the chapel before the bell struck the hour, but no words of persuasion on the part of the two *Bibis* could induce them to arise and walk.

The minutes ticked on. The atmosphere in the chapel grew tense. The *Bibis,* having exhausted all known means to induce the brides to move, resorted to threats. At last the *Bwana,* speaking a few heated words to the bridegrooms outside the chapel door, walked up the path with long strides, but when he saw the brides followed by the *Bibis* moving in the direction of the chapel a few steps at a time, he returned in silence to wait at his post.

The behavior of the brides was good form in the Kikuyu way of weddings. A Kikuyu bride is seized in her garden, on the path, or by a stream with her waterpot and carried away to the groom's village by a band of his young warrior friends. Here her girl friends come every evening for a week to weep and wail with her over the fact that her girlhood has ended. A few weeks later, when she is taken to visit her mother by one of the female relatives of the groom, she hangs her head and looks at the ground, takes hold of the end of a slender stick by which she is pulled a few steps at a time until she reaches the mother's dwelling. It required hours and sometimes days of patient waiting between her halts to take a bride to visit her mother, but patience is a virtue, and time has no value in Kikuyuland.

When the girls finally reached the chapel door, the *Bibis* pushed them into position to move down the aisle with the wedding party, while the congregation sang a Kikuyu translation of "Love Divine, All Loves Excelling," and thus dispelled the troubled atmosphere which had prevailed.

The *Bwana* proceeded with the wedding in perfect Kikuyu and had arrived at the point where the brides were to respond to their vows. The grooms had responded to the questions asked of them, but the brides were silent. The *Bwana* repeated the questions twice, but there was no response. The poor dears were too frightened and confused by the ways of the *athungu* (white people) to utter a sound. The ceremony proceeded with the grooms taking all responsibility "until death us do part." Then the *Bwana* was asking for the rings.

"With this ring do I thee wed," said Johana, producing Keige's ring.

Paul fumbled through his pockets but could not locate Njeri's ring. Had he left it in his hut? Had Njoroge, who was examining it carefully last night, returned it? These and many other similar questions raced through his excited brain as he stood there searching frantically. The congregation waited in breathless silence. The ring was found in the nick of time between the folds of the lining of his pocket and produced to form the last tie in the knot which joined Paul to Njeri in Christian wedlock.

The *Bwana's* face was hot and flushed when he pronounced them man and wife and offered a prayer of blessing. He led the way to a table on the side where they signed the Government register. Their marriage would be recorded at the Government post in accord with a law recently laid down. Christian marriage was making its mark on Kikuyu life. The boys who were being given a Christian marriage here and there throughout the tribe would think twice before they allowed thoughts of buying a second wife to overcome them.

The congregation had left their seats to go outside while the register was being signed. In their hands they held petals and heads of flowers with which they pelted the wedding group as they emerged from the door. The brides and grooms, solemn and silent, moved with their attendants up the path toward the place where the wedding feast had been prepared. The crowd that followed them had cast all restraint to the winds and were out for a day of fun.

Only invited guests took their places at the tables which had been arranged in the black wattle grove. The crowd stood around the edges to see this first exhibition of the affair of the marriage of the people of God in their midst. Huge plates of rice with a curried meat and potato stew were served. This was followed by bananas and tea with plenty of sugar. By way of entertainment the mission boys staged a game of football on the playgrounds in the afternoon. The wedding party with their friends went to look on and cheer.

It was the time of the full moon. The day's festivities were over. The black wattle trees in the grove, where the wedding feast had been spread, silhouetted against the moonlit sky, threw black velvet shadows across the path leading down to the new house which had been built at Matara. The girls were escorting Keige to her new home. Njeri was with them. I watched them as they went down the path moving in and out of the patches of bright moonlight and deep shadows. Probably shadows would fall across the road that stretched through the years ahead of them.

"Thank God," I said to myself, "they know the Light of the world. He will walk with them as they walk through the shadows and will bring light out of darkness. 'He that followeth me, shall not walk in darkness.' "

The group of girls separated when they reached Keige's house. Part of them escorted Keige over her new threshold; the others went with Njeri to temporary quarters which had been prepared for her and Paul. Tomorrow they would journey over the ridges to their new home near Kahora's village. The girls removed the brides' veils and assisted them to settle into their new quarters. Good nights were said, and with great gaiety they returned to the girls' house, their happy, overflowing spirits expressing themselves in bursts of Kikuyu and mission songs.

Perhaps the brides and grooms with their Christian friends had not fully understood the significance of the day, but it was the beginning of a new era. In the heart of pagan, polygamous Kikuyuland two family altars would be established. One father and one mother would gather children around the fire in the middle of the earth floor and there, by the flickering firelight, they would read the words of the Book of God and pray to the Author and Finisher of their faith. Who could measure the influence of Christian homes scattered throughout the tribe, homes founded and maintained by Christian fathers and mothers, homes from which the stifling, dwarfing, deadening influence of heathenism would be banished—unknown and unfelt?

Chapter 13

BURIED

CHANGES WERE SCHEDULED to take place shortly on most of our Kikuyu stations. The last mail had brought the *Bwana* a letter requesting him to return to Kijabe to take over the home side of the Rift Valley Academy, the school for missionary children. If he agreed to go, another missionary couple would be asked to take charge of the Matara work. *Bibi* McKinstry was to go to America soon.

The McKenricks decided to take up the work at the Academy. Busy days followed their decision. A number of the Matara boys had entered the catechumen class to prepare for baptism before the *Bwana* left for Kijabe and soon after for the homeland. Now they had completed their two years of instruction. Wambui and Keige also were ready for baptism. *Bwana* McKenrick planned a baptismal service for the Sunday before *Bibi* McKinstry left for furlough.

Out across the morning sunlit air that Sunday sounded the clear peals of the chapel bell. Brown figures dressed in khaki shorts and white muslin shirts emerged from the various boys' huts below the chapel. Down the broad main path leading from the hilltop came the pad of the girls' brown feet. The *Bwana* and the three *Bibis* followed them. Some of the boys and several of the girls carried bundles of clothing tied up by the four corners of a large kerchief. The bundles contained the clean, fresh clothing to be worn by those who were to be baptized. They were carried by the friends of the candidates for baptism who would help them change from their wet, dripping clothes to the dry ones.

A quiet hush fell over the small company that sat in the chapel and listened to the *Bwana's* words as he explained from the Book of God the significance of baptism. They were buried with Christ by baptism unto death. If they were planted together with Him in the likeness of death, they should also live in the likeness of His resurrection. Should they then continue in sin? God forbid. How should they that died to sin live any longer in it? Were they not therefore now called upon to reckon themselves dead unto sin, and would they not be able to reign over sin through the Lord Jesus Christ who now lived within them and thus to walk with Him in newness of life day by day?

The chapel service was over. The congregation formed a procession and moved in the direction of the Nyakibai, the waters of which had been dammed up to form a baptismal pool. There were five candidates for baptism. As they neared the river, they disappeared from the crowd with their attendants. The girls went to a thicket to the right of the path, the boys to the left, where they changed to the clothing in which they would descend to the waters. The *Bwana,* staff in hand, stepped down into the quiet waters of the pool. People from the surrounding villages came from the bushes and walked down the paths to mingle with the mission people and to ask the meaning of this new affair of the river. The candidates walked down the paths leading from their bushy dressing rooms and stood in line on the bank of the river. As they did so, their Christian friends burst forth in song,

Kwi na ruui rua thakame . . .

There is a fountain filled with blood
Drawn from Immanuel's veins;
And sinners, plunged beneath that flood,
Lose all their guilty stains.

Back from the hills came the echo in reply, "Lose all their guilty stains." As the echo was carried down the ridges on the ethereal waves by a gentle breeze, the first boy in line stepped into the waters to take his place by the *Bwana's* side. The next moment he was plunged beneath the quiet waters of the Nyakibai to signify a humble believer's identification with the Christ of Calvary in his death and resurrection and the laying aside of the old life to put on the new.

Who can forget the scene or the presence of the Spirit of God as He manifested Himself in these black-skinned disciples, aglow with a new-found joy?

"Did the *Bwana* say you were buried?" asked one of the recently arrived girls of Wambui that evening as they sat by the fire.

"Yes, buried with *Kristo,*" replied Wambui thoughtfully, "a *ngerekano* [illustration] of the affair which God has done through *Jesu Kristo.* Not only my sins were all buried with Him, but also those of all who will believe in Him."

"*Kai,* the affair of God is *munene* [great]!" exclaimed the girl with eyes that opened wide as she caught a faint glimpse of the truth and results of the incarnation, death, and resurrection of the Son of God.

"So great is the affair which is being preached to us that it made *Jesu* leave His throne to die on the cross, and, too, it has made these white people to leave their homes across the waters and live in our bushes to teach us about Him. *Kai, tiitheru* [of a truth], the affair of God is very powerful," said Wambui seriously. Her grasp of the truth of the Gospel could be explained only by the presence of a Teacher from Heaven who abode at Matara to guide all who believed on the One who is the truth.

"I pray not that thou shouldest take them out of the world, but that thou shouldest keep them from the evil. . . . Sanctify them through thy truth. . . . As thou hast sent me into the world, even so have I also sent them into the world." So prayed the Saviour for the three boys and two girls who that day were buried with Him in baptism and who would go forth to take their places and live their lives among their own people.

KINYONA
1916, 1917

Chapter 14

NEW HORIZONS

NEARLY FOUR YEARS had rolled around since I had crossed the Nyakibai River on the back of a tired mule and caught my first glimpse of Matara station. The African boys and girls with their teachers who had lived and worked together to carry the Light of the world into the darkness of Matara district were soon to scatter in many directions. The girls' house of corrugated iron was to be taken down and rebuilt at Githumu, where an experienced worker who knew African girls and was well acquainted with their ways and the means of dealing with them had been appointed to take charge of them.

The senior *Bibi* would take the path which led through the deep wide seas to furlough. The McKenricks had moved back to Kijabe, and the belongings of the missionaries who were to take their place had begun to arrive at Matara. I had received notice to proceed to Kinyona, where the *Bibi* Collins was left alone because her fellow missionaries had developed a serious illness and been ordered home.

When I took Kihoga and left for Kinyona astride Ndeithia, we took Wanjiru with us, for she and Kihoga had been married by the *Bwana* before he left for Kijabe. The end of the long rainy season was at hand, and the day was quite an ordinary one for that time of year. For five months the glorious African sun had been shrouded in heavy clouds and blankets of fog, but for several days now the ceiling had been higher than usual and was marked by lines of light. Today there were deep rifts in the steel-gray dome. By ten o'clock the clouds seemed to be rolling themselves into bundles in preparation to depart. They moved slowly over the ridges and valleys toward Ukambaland. By midday floods of sunshine burst forth across the landscape now and again, only to be overtaken, pushed back, and veiled again by slow-moving billows of clouds. A titanic struggle was going on in the regions above us. Would sunshine or shadow, light or darkness, conquer Kikuyuland?

My eyes roamed down the parallel ridges stretching away to the southeast to melt in the Ukamba plains. All Kikuyuland was one patchwork of sunshine and shadow. The clouds were high, the bundles tighter, the spaces between were widening. The sun was gaining an advantage, and the air was crystal clear.

Many times during the four years at Matara, clouds and fogs had descended upon the trio who were traveling today. We had walked through mists and darkness. Oftentimes we had not been able to see our way clearly, but as we had waited in faith and hope, the sun would break through, roll up the clouds and fog banks, toss them over the edges of the horizon, and remain to gladden and make bright the days to follow. Many clouds had tightened over the Matara Ridge only to part and make room for the sunshine. In time would all the ridges before us be filled with bright patches of light?

By four o'clock in the afternoon, eighty miles away, Mount Kenya, queen of mountains, emerged from the clouds in all of her majestic beauty.

"Do you know the Kikuyu name for that mountain?" asked Kihoga as he walked by the side of the mule. "It is *Kere-Nyaga,* and it means 'the mountain having brightness.' The Agikuyu believe the mountain is the earthly dwelling place of Ngai

[God]. They say that Ngai lives in the sky, but that He comes to the mountain from time to time to bring punishment or blessing to the people."

"Do the Agikuyu pray to Ngai?"

"Yes, when they offer their sacrifices, they raise their hands and face Kere-Nyaga. A Mugikuyu does not pray by himself. The family must gather together to pray when the help of Ngai is wanted. When it thunders, the Agikuyu say that Ngai is cracking his joints to make ready to destroy His enemies. They believe the lightning is one of His weapons used in warfare. They believe it is a very dangerous affair to look up to the heavens when it thunders. If people are struck by lightning, the Agikuyu say it is because they looked up and it made Ngai very angry. Mothers tell their children to go into the hut when they hear thunder and never to look up at the clouds."

"Only God, by His Spirit, can help the Agikuyu to know and believe the truth about Himself," I commented.

"Have you heard that Johana and Keige are leaving Matara?" I asked as we crossed the last river and were about to climb the last ridge that separated us from Kinyona.

"I heard Johana say they were moving to his father's village between Matara and Kijabe."

"Johana says the people of his district have not heard the words of God. He wants to build the first outschool, explain to them the affairs of the true God, and teach them to read the Word of God for themselves. No doubt this is God's method for sending the light of the Gospel to all the dark places of Kikuyuland."

When the missionaries first invaded Kikuyuland, Karanja had been the great chief in the large district which we were entering, and when Charles E. Hurlburt traveled through the Fort Hall district in search of a site for a mission station, Karanja's son, Njiri, was assisting his father to rule the Agikuyu and direct their affairs. Hearing of the white man's desire,

Njiri made a two days' journey to contact the *Bwana* Hurlburt and invite him to open a mission station near his village. In response, Mr. Hurlburt chose Kinyona, and Njiri gave him the plot on which to establish the station. Karanja died soon after that, and Njiri, who inherited the chieftainship while still a young man, continued to look with favor on the new *miceni.*

Kinyona was a gloomy station in those days, before the buildings were pulled apart and carried by sections to the highest ridge, there to be rebuilt on an inspiring site overlooking all Kikuyuland. When I came from Matara with Kihoga and Wanjiru, they were still on the original site in a depression between the ridges with hills on all sides. The combination chapel and school was made of wooden slabs and grass thatch. The long rambling dwelling house was built of boards loosely joined together and roofed with grass. It was set on poles, in lieu of a foundation, and when the rains were on and the ground was soft and water-soaked, the weight of the house sank some of the poles farther into the ground than others, making the floor-level precarious. Sometimes the doors in one end of the house could not be closed, while those in the other end could not be opened, and vice versa. When it rained hard, the residents slept under umbrellas and placed pails on their beds to catch the drip in the places unprotected by the umbrellas.

It was into this home that the *Bibi* Collins, overjoyed to meet a friend who would share her joys and sorrows, welcomed me that evening, and I settled down for a well-earned night's rest in the east bedroom, which was to be my inner sanctum for the next year and a half.

"Njiri, the chief, has come to greet you," announced Kihoga the following morning as the two *Bibis* were eating their breakfast.

Njiri was garbed in a gorgeous full-length robe of coney skins, which extended to within nine inches of the ground.

The long, shiny white fur of a colobus monkey fell from his left shoulder in regal splendor. His head was closely shaven. Small round wires strung with pink and blue beads decorated the holes in the top cartilages of his ears, while curved iron drops tipped with small balls of bright copper hung from the large holes in the lobes. He carried a long, highly polished walking stick with a curved ball on the end, a token of prestige which Kikuyu custom permitted only to those whose wisdom and position in the tribe warranted it.

At this time Njiri had forty wives and was regarded by Government officials to be one of the most aggressive and reliable chiefs in all that region. I took note of his regal bearing that morning, and when he began to speak, I knew by the tone of his voice and by his decisive way of talking that he was the possessor of a powerful personality.

"I have come to greet the *mugeni* [the stranger]," said he as he shook the new *Bibi's* hand.

Then he grabbed her thumb, at which point she knew it was in order for her to grasp his thumb, ending with a final shake of the hand. This performance the chief initiated three times to emphasize its warmth. It was the authentic Kikuyu greeting of friendship—and a friendship it proved to be, of long duration and unique understanding, for Njiri and the *Bibi* were the kind of friends whose divergent principles led them into frequent tiffs and clashes with one another, yet who could survive the bouts with mutual respect and good will.

"Njiri is a good friend to us," put in the *Bibi* Collins, who stood by viewing the introduction with satisfaction. "When we need an extra mule or porters, we call upon him, and he always helps us out."

"The Kinyona station is here because I wanted it to come," Njiri reinforced the compliment. "When *Bwana* Hurlburt rode through these bushes looking for a place to build his mission, did he not come to me? Did I not give him this *githaka* [this plot of land]? Did I not say to him, 'Build here'? *Tiitheru* [of a truth], I am a friend of the mission.

"Abide in peace, I go to a *cira* [a court case]," he said after exchanging a few more words with the *Bibis*. Then he bowed and turned down the path.

"I suppose we should have a little talk about the planning of our work," said the *Bibi* Collins later as we sat by a table in the rambling house. "I have been teaching the station school and spending part of my time visiting the people in their villages. We have two outschools attached to this station. One is at Icamaguthi, in charge of your Kihoga's half brother, Thaiti. Warimwe teaches in the other one, at Gathukiini. Would you like to supervise these two schools? And could you teach the catechumen class and do the medical work here on the station, too?"

It was a large order, but there were only the two of us to carry it all; I must do my share.

Chapter 15

DIFFUSING LIGHT

THE FOLLOWING MONDAY found me astride Ndeithia, led by Kihoga, making our way through the mist and cold of the high altitude to Icamaguthi. There we found Thaiti in charge of a group of bright boys from the surrounding villages. The boys were clad in a part of the dressed skin of a goat or a yard of unbleached muslin thrown over their shoulders. They compressed themselves into as small a space as they could occupy, folding their arms and legs close to their bodies, warming one body part with another, for the room was bare and cold.

Thaiti was teaching a few who had mastered the syllables and were being launched into the mysteries of reading the first small book. The most advanced pupil in the school was struggling to teach a class of beginners to read the syllables. The reading lesson over, I gave them a lesson on Jesus, the Light of the world, who is the way to the village of God.

"Oh, yes," said the bright little boys with smiling faces, "we want His light to shine in our hearts, and we want to walk with Him in His path."

An hour's ride from Icamaguthi brought us to Warimwe's school at Gathukiini. Here among the herdboys we found a class of about a dozen girls between the ages of ten and twelve.

This was most unusual. At Matara no one ever had been able to induce any of the village girls to come to school. The women had told them they never would give birth to a child if they touched the affair of school—a thoroughly effective warning in Kikuyuland. These Gathukiini girls were keen. They answered intelligently the questions that we asked them about the way of salvation. They seemed to be following the light that had been given to them. Warimwe was leading them on with great zeal.

"Knowing the ways of the enemy, I cannot help wondering what plot he will invent to try to turn these children back to darkness. We must pray much for them," I told Kihoga as we journeyed home.

"*Hodi, hodi* [may I come in]?" called a masculine voice outside the kitchen door one day soon after this first visit to the outschools.

It was Mucai, a youth whose village was a stone's throw from the mission but with whom as yet I had slight acquaintance. His sister was one of several young unmarried girls who occupied a hut on the edge of the station while they learned more of the affair of God which was pulling them from the darkness of Kikuyuland.

"This small girl is my sister," he said, pointing to a wisp of a child about five years of age, clad in a three-by-two-inch leather apron tied around her waist by a leather string. "Will you take her and look after her?"

The bacon-colored little Nyambura was covered with goose flesh, and shivered as the cold, foggy winds blew about her fragile body.

"Come in," I invited, leading them to some African stools near the fire, where they could be comfortable as they talked.

"After my father's death," began Mucai, "it was my affair to find rupees to pay the hut taxes for our village. I went to work for a white man on the plateau, but when the dysentery sickness carried away many Kinyona people, my relatives sent for me to come home to see my sick mother. When I arrived, they pointed to the bushes. She was dead. It is the affair of the oldest son to bury the father or mother,[1] but I feared to go near death. I had refused to listen to the words of God because I wanted to follow the dances of the Agikuyu, but I went to *Bibi* Collins at the mission for help then. Kamau, Thaiti, and Warimwe came to the bushes. They dug a grave and buried my mother, and they prayed that we would believe the words of *Jesu.* As for me, I sat far away in the bushes watching and thinking.

" 'Why do these boys not fear death?' I asked myself. 'They were born in Kikuyuland and taught to believe all the things of fear which I have been taught, yet they are not eaten by fear as I am today. I will go to the mission. I want to be like them.'

"On the next day that comes out of the week,[2] I came to the mission to hear the words of God, and I stood in the meeting to say I was believing in *Jesu.* Now I want to go to school that I may learn to read the words of God, but what shall I do with Nyambura?"

"She may live in the hut with her sister and go to the morning school," I said, rejoicing to hear the story of the light breaking in another Kikuyu heart as it had come about shortly before my arrival at Kinyona.

"I have never seen such an interest in school at Kinyona," said the *Bibi* Collins one day during midterm. "I really do not know how to manage all the pupils. I have put all the boys who can read to teaching, and still the classes are overcrowded. Do you know, I believe that Mucai will make a teacher. He is reading already and does very well in all his work. You would

[1]Kikuyu dead were buried only if survived by a son who was old enough to perform the duty.
[2]Sunday.

enjoy hearing little Nyambura say Bible verses. She can repeat all the verses given the beginners to learn."

"Mucai wants you to lend him your lantern," announced Ngoni, the small houseboy, as he appeared in the doorway one night after he had finished his evening chores. "Many of the village boys come to his hut. He is teaching them the affair of reading, but they cannot see well. Is it not a good affair for Mucai to do this? He teaches them to sing the songs of God, too."

"I hear your brother, who cooks for Lord Delamere in Nairobi, has come to your home at Mununga for a holiday."

"Yes, and he says he will not return. He has been pulled by the words of Mucai to learn to read and to leave the ways of Nairobi to walk in the path of God."

"Are you and this brother from Nairobi of one father?"

"Yes, but we are not of one mother. The father of Kihugu, the person of God from Mununga who sometimes goes to Kijabe for your loads of food, and our father had one father—and he was a landowner." The last remark was made with pride, for in the Kikuyu system of land tenure, the landowner was highly respected as a peer among his less well-to-do tenants.

"*Kai ni atia* [what is the matter]?" shouted an irritated voice from the darkness. "Have you forgotten you were sent to borrow the *Bibi's* lantern? Can the boys in Mucai's hut learn to read without a light?"

Ngoni seized the lantern he had lit and ran along the bush path, knowing he would receive a tongue lashing when he arrived.

"Ndingori, the cook, has left us and gone to his faraway village. *Bibi* Collins is busy with her school, and I have to go to the outschools. Who will cook our food today?" I asked Ngoni one blue Monday morning when everything seemed to go wrong.

"I think my brother Mwenja will come if you ask him."

"Does he know how to cook European food?"

"Yes, is it not he who cooked for Lord Delamere in Nairobi?"

A few hours later Mwenja walked into the kitchen, tied the strings of an apron behind him, and took over. One domestic problem thus successfully solved, another was to confront us.

"Your cows have eaten my maize stalks and yam vines six times, and I have forgiven you, but this time you pay a fine," said a village man as he met the *Bibis* on the path.

"That herdboy is far too irresponsible to be trusted," admitted one of the *Bibis*. "We must look for another, and we will send the elders to judge the affair of the garden and tell us what we are to pay you."

"Come, the *Bibi* wants to speak to you," called Ngoni the following day as his relative Kihugu passed by.

"Could you find a good herder for us?" I asked him, knowing I could trust his judgment. "Our herdboy allows the cows to go into the Agikuyu gardens. We are in much trouble because of this affair."

"I think," replied Kihugu quietly after some moments of turning the matter over in his mind. "I think my relative Thiga would come. He is a *mwanake* [young man], and is very wise in the affairs of cows."

"Tell him to come."

So Thiga came, and he proved to be indeed a young man who was "very wise in the affairs of cows"—so wise in fact, that his heart was to go wholly and solely after the affair of cows until he possessed a herd of large cattle interbred with European stock that greatly enhanced his prestige when he had come into his rights as a landowner on Mununga Ridge. But the *Bibis* did not foresee that distant day or the sorrows that would follow Thiga and his cattle, so we were well pleased now that his wisdom was put to good use in guiding our cows to good feeding grounds, keeping them out of the gardens of the Agikuyu, and seeing that we had always a good supply of milk and butter. This service Thiga performed with fidelity, and he became a cheerful carrier of loads as well when the *Bibis* sallied forth on safaris through Kikuyuland.

Sunday after Sunday the young men from Mucai's night class arose in the morning services to confess their faith in Jesus Christ as Saviour. Then they joined the catechumen class to receive instruction for baptism. What a class it was! There was Gacingiri who had spent a term in jail and had learned to use marijuana on a settler's farm upcountry where he was employed. He was saved and delivered by the grace of God. There was our cook Mwenja, and his little brother Ngoni our houseboy from Mununga; Kuria and his wife Ndono; Ngahu and Gituara and the sons of Chief Njiri's prime minister, a very influential Kikuyu elder of the district; and many other of the school children.

Mucai made such rapid progress in school that *Bibi* Collins had given him a class of beginners. On Sunday afternoons he was always to be found down the ridge at Mathanjiini with a group of schoolboys, surrounded by the local people. They taught them to sing the songs of God in the Kikuyu tongue, explained the meaning of the hymns, and exhorted them to believe on the Son of God. Interest increased until they said they would build a chapel-school if Mucai would come to teach them to read.

"*Kai,* can we remember the words of God if we do not hear them many times?" they argued.

"The people of my village at Mununga want you to send them a teacher. We will build a building. Will you send us someone?" asked Thiga the herdman, though he himself was never to leave the ways of the Agikuyu to follow the light he had seen.

"Dear me," I said, "how will we answer all these calls? We

will have to see the chiefs and the landowners to ask if they are willing for the people to have schools."

"Oh, Njiri will not refuse," said the Christian boys; "he also wants to learn to read. He is going to build a school near his village. He wants you to send a teacher to teach his boys. He will join the class when he is not away in Government service."

Life bristled with interest at Kinyona when the next term opened. Mucai was chosen to teach in the new bush school at Mathanjiini. Kamati, the most advanced pupil, had studied at Kinyona. Now he was enthusiastic in recruiting scholars from his own area and was helping to teach. Kihoga had helped the Mununga people to build their school and was filling in as teacher. Njiri's school was finished also. Kariuki, an evangelist sent from Kijabe, was there. So I had five outschools now to visit and supervise. On a visit to Njiri's school, I listened to Kariuki teach the Bible lesson at the close of the morning session. The chief himself was there and listened most attentively.

"Njiri," I asked him, "what do you think about the good news of salvation we teach you to believe and receive?"

"I believe it is all true," he replied solemnly. "I believe *Jesu* was the Son of God and came to this world as you say. I know I am not a good man. I know if I believe and follow Him, He will take me to His village."

"Njiri," pleaded Kariuki, who had joined us, "will you not trust the Lord *Jesu* to wash away your sins with His blood? He says He will remember them against you no more forever. Will you receive Him now and confess Him before men?"

Tense moments followed. The chief drew a long breath and clasped his head in his hands as light struggled with darkness, flesh with spirit.

"What shall I do about all my wives? What could I do when the Agikuyu bring me much beer? How could I carry on my business with Government? No, I am too entangled by the affairs of the Agikuyu," he said at last.

Had Njiri made the decision that day to follow the path which his own lips had confessed to be right, one thunderous clash between the forces of darkness and light at Kinyona might have been averted.

Chapter 16

THE LIGHT STRIKES AN AGE-OLD CUSTOM

THE LIGHT GREEN of the growing *mukombi* (the millet) on the long rectangular spaces of the hillsides near the Gathukiini outschool looked like a huge patchwork quilt as it grew between rectangular spaces of dark green potato vines. When the *mukombi* was knee-high, the boys and girls would begin their precircumcision dances to prepare them for one of the greatest events in the life of a young Mugikuyu. For three months the candidates for circumcision would sing and dance the circumcision dance, *kuhura.* They would dance it when they reached the wide open spaces on the ridge paths. They would dance near the markets and before the villages of rich men. Everywhere they would be hailed with shouts of welcome and given an abundance of all the delicacies of Kikuyuland.

In the Kikuyu tribe the circumcision of boys and girls marked the passage from childhood to adulthood. The age groups upon which tribal life and rights to administration are built were formed the day on which the circumcision operation was performed. From this beginning, the Agikuyu passed with their age groups through an intricate series of promotions which entitled and obligated them to fulfill their duties, both civic and religious, that were necessary to their closely knit communal life. Could it have been stripped of those practices which were contrary to the light of the knowledge of God, the organization and discipline of these age groups on which all tribal life was built would have been highly commendable as well as efficient and practical.

The Kikuyu child, from nine or ten years up, received much instruction concerning the rules of conduct, tribal tradition, and religion. As they neared the age of puberty, the elders took more time to instruct the circumcision candidates thoroughly concerning the practices, responsibilities, beliefs, and various duties expected of them as they entered adulthood and the state of full membership in the Kikuyu tribe, making sure that they received specific teaching concerning the circumstances attending the natural propagation of life.

Marriage and the production of children—which gave the Agikuyu added privilege and standing in the tribe as they became successively parents, parents of a circumcised child, and grandparents—were contingent upon the all-important entrance into adult status by means of circumcision and its attendant ceremonies. Disturbing psychological factors inevitably complicated this critical moment of life. Certain forms of license were permitted. There were few if any restraining influences brought to bear upon the initiates by parents or older people concerned. For certain months after the initiation ceremonies, boys and girls were not expected to do work of any kind. They roamed the countryside together, were feted joyfully, and received wherever they chose to go.

Initiation ceremonies for Kikuyu boys involved much that was both mentally and morally degrading. The initiation of Kikuyu girls included very harmful and painful mutilation of the generative organs. Sometimes death followed, and permanent disabilities always. In times of childbirth, labor was delayed, and often as a consequence both mother and child died under tragic circumstances. The group of schoolgirls at Gathukiini were in grave danger when the *mukombi* reached knee height and their contemporaries began to dance the *kuhura.* They had given their hearts to *Jesu.* They were thrilled by the Christian way of life—and the end of the Christian life, did it not lead to the village of God? Did not the verses they recited tell them *Jesu* was the Door of entrance into that village? Did they want Him to say to them, when He came again, "I never knew you: depart from me"? No, they had heard Him say, "Come unto me," and they had come. They would not leave Him and His path to return to the path of the Agikuyu.

The Gathukiini schoolgirls told their mothers they did not want to dance the *kuhura* or be circumcised. They then were called before their fathers to be reasoned with. Did they not know that girls uncircumcised before they became women were unclean and were cut off from the Kikuyu tribe? They would become barren and the great Kikuyu tribe would be no more. To all the arguments, the girls said quietly:

"*Aca, tutikwenda* [no, we do not want it]."

"Girls are the property of their fathers," shouted one old father. "We do not follow the affairs of *comba* [the palefaces]. You will have to be circumcised. Return to your mothers' huts that they may instruct you how to become the mothers of many children."

Warimwe was in great distress the next time he came in from Gathukiini.

"The parents have taken their girls from school against their wills to be circumcised," he reported solemnly. "They have been subjected to many heathen customs of sin. Perhaps they will never return to us again."

After forced instruction and preparation, the girls had been pulled from their mothers' huts and led down to the river in the early dawn to walk out into the ice-cold water to their waists with the other candidates to numb their bodies. They had been followed by a crowd of eager spectators who also followed them later up the hill to an open space on the ridge. Shouts and trills had heralded the appearance of the boys' circumciser followed by the old woman who was to operate upon the girls. After the operation the girls had been led to a special hut and tended there in seclusion by their sponsors. The ceremonies that had followed lasted for many days.

The first group of young Kikuyu girls to make an effort to leave the path of ignorance, superstition, and bondage to walk with the Light of the world in the path of freedom and truth had been overcome and thwarted. Would discouragement overcome them? Would they abandon all hope to sink back into the darkness of Kikuyu life? Or having tasted the good things of the Christian, would they return to walk with the Saviour in His path?

"We must trust to the words they have heard to lead them back to the path of light," I told Warimwe, confident that darkness could not hold those who were truly illuminated within by the Light of life.

Another series of events was taking place on the Kinyona Ridge about this time, the central figure of which was to play an important part in days to come, not only in my personal life and work, but in Kikuyu politics—but if I knew Muthungu then it was only as one of the scantily dressed herdboys with which the Kinyona school was overflowing during this time of prosperity, and there was nothing about him distinguishing enough to bring his name to my mind as a live memory of those Kinyona days. Yet hearing the whole story in detail from his own lips in later years, it is easy to reconstruct it.

The sun was sinking slowly toward the tops of the banana trees on the brow of a Kikuyu ridge. A tall old man with long, thin legs, a rectangular garment of goatskins tied over one shoulder, a cap of woolly white sheepskin on his head, and a long staff in his hand stood on a ridge path near Kinyona. He waved his long staff in the direction of his village as he called to Muthungu, his son, herding the flock of sheep and goats that were feeding in the valley and on the slopes of the ridge.

"*Riua riguthua* [the sun is setting]," he called. "It is time to take the flocks home."

With a shrill whistle and a shepherd's call, Muthungu rounded up the animals, calling to his younger brother to lead the flock to their village while he followed behind to encourage the stragglers to fall in line. Njuguna, the old father of the boys, brought up the rear while his eagle eye followed the long line of sheep and goats to make sure they were all there. Three of his wives moved in and out of their individual huts. The other three, Muthungu's mother among them, had gone to the spirit world. If the sweet-potato vines for the sheep to feed upon were not hanging on the pegs in each woman's hut when the flocks came home, they knew a storm would break.

Njuguna was respected and feared by all members of his village. Until recent days no one had ever thought of disputing his word, which was law. Now the two boys were in disfavor because they had a great desire to go to Kinyona mission school to learn to read. Many a night they had been thrust out into the outside grain bin to sleep in the cold without food to cure them of their desire to leave the path of Kikuyu boys for the affairs of the white man. This evening they ate their evening meal of cooked corn and beans with their father as they sat with him around the fire the women had built on the hard clay floor of the *thingira,* as the men's hut was called.

"Is it not time for you to go to Nairobi to look for work?" asked the boys' father, addressing Muthungu.

"*Kai njui* [do I know]?" replied Muthungu.

"Why do you not know? You know some day you will be asking me for sheep to buy a wife. It is time for you to bring shillings to the village to buy those sheep," said the shrewd old man.

Muthungu had learned to read by finding some other herdboy to take over his flock until after school hours on days when his father went off to the beer drinks. He had a great desire to follow the affair of school, and now his father was commanding him to look for work. Two weeks later he set off with a companion for Nairobi. There they secured work as kitchen boys in a hotel where a Kinyona man was employed as cook.

After six months Muthungu returned to his village to hand over to his father his hard-earned shillings—barring the price of his two shirts and the pair of shorts he was wearing. The evening after his arrival, a band of boys of his own age from the district came to the village to greet him. Their nude bodies and faces were plastered with white clay in which fantastic patterns had been drawn. Feathers were attached to their hair. They wore girdles of reeds. Large circles of twisted dry vines hung around their necks. A narrow crown of dried weeds adorned each head. They carried shields made of zebra or other skins. Muthungu laughed as they approached the village. He knew they had come to lure him away to dress him in the same garb, thus to witness to the Kikuyu world their desire to be circumcised and qualify as members of the tribe. He chatted with them, but when they urged him to join them, he told them he had not fully made up his mind.

Muthungu had an older brother of another mother, Gituero, one of the strongest Christians among the Kinyona young men. The morning after the visit of the boys, Gituero sought out Muthungu.

"I hear the boys of your age group were in the village last night," he said. "Before you went to Nairobi, did you not tell me you wanted to know the affair of school and follow the path of a person of God? You are now standing at the parting of the two paths. You can choose the path of a pagan Kikuyu, or if you choose to be a man of God, go to the mission station and ask the *Bwana* of the hospital to circumcise you."

The boy who had not been present with his age group to receive his tribal education around the evening fires from the old elders in the months prior to circumcision would be ridiculed by members of his age group and said to be an ignoramus. Apart from the initiation ceremonies, there was no recognition of adulthood and its responsibilities among his people. Muthungu knew all this and went out into the bushes alone to make his decision after this talk with Gituero. He was the possessor of a proud spirit. Could he face the ridicule of his age group throughout the years if he went to the mission for circumcision? Tears filled his eyes, but after a long struggle and a prayer to God for help, he made his final decision. A week later Muthungu was circumcised by the mission doctor. Another young Mugikuyu had turned his back at the crossroads on the path of darkness to follow the path of light.

Chapter 17

THE PINCH OF WAR

"THE MAIL HAS JUST COME in from Kijabe," said the *Bibi* Collins one day as I arrived from a trip to the outschools. The news is rather disturbing. Nairobi officials have discovered that German East Africa[1] is preparing to invade British East Africa. Orders have gone out to the settlers here to organize an army to go against them. The District Commissioners are being asked to recruit Africans from all the districts to go with the army to do porterage."

"That might mean that we will feel the pinch of the war even here," I replied solemnly.

Indeed, we were to feel the pinch of more than one war. The witch doctors, whose business it was to keep in touch with the Kikuyu spirit world to divine and advise on any course of action, were warning the tribal elders that something must be done to keep the boys and girls from going to mission schools. If they followed the new ideas and customs that the white man was teaching them, many disasters would come to the Kikuyu ridges. The rains would fail; famine would overtake them; disease would carry away the people and their cattle. The elders, taking these warnings to heart, were bringing their influence to bear on the subchiefs. The Christians at Kinyona

[1]Now the British Mandate of Tanganyika.

could feel the pressure of the powers of darkness operating all about them.

Every week the District Commissioner sent orders to the chiefs to draft more young Agikuyu to go to German East Africa as porters for the army. At first the schoolboys were exempt. Then pagan boys who had no desire to leave the paths of heathendom came to the schools to avoid going to war, which incensed the tribal elders more than ever. We obtained an agreement with the D. C. that the chiefs were not to touch the schoolboys who had been in school before the war broke out. When the schoolboys were wanted, he said, he would ask the mission to give him a list of their names and the date of their enrollment. Those who had read the longest would be the last to be taken. Still there was constant friction with the subchiefs who interrupted our schools seeking ways to seize the Christian boys.

"The herdboys are coming to learn to read, even though some of the fathers seek to prevent them," reported Mucai on one of his visits to us. "Kamati learns very fast. He helps me to teach the *toto* [the young boys]. They can repeat many verses from the Book of God, and they know to explain the meaning, too. But Njiri's subchief at Mathanjiini is opposed to our school. Someone told me he is planning to seize the schoolboys and send them to war as porters."

On a Sunday noon about six weeks later, an excited group of young Africans burst into the mission station led by Mucai.

"*Bibi,*" he cried, "Njiri's subchief and his men broke up our service this morning. They seized some of our boys. Kamati was one. They've taken them to Fort Hall to be sent to war. They had no right to take Kamati. If they want porters, let them take their own boys who have come lately into the school to hide. *Bibi,* write a letter to the D. C. Tell him Kamati was the first boy to believe and come to school."

"Calm yourselves," I said, waving my hand to quiet the upset boys. "I will go up and speak to Njiri about the matter."

Njiri was in the midst of a beer drink with his subchiefs and council members. He left the group and came over to greet me when he saw me standing in the path. Stating my case, I reminded him of the Government agreement in regard to the schoolboys, suggesting by way of tact that he might be unaware of this. Would he please see that Kamati was rescued and brought back to school? The chief's senses were so dulled by drink that his usual diplomatic approach to such a situation was lacking. Clad in his regal fur robe, he reared his head, straightened his body to full height, and waved his wand of authority in the direction of the Kikuyu ridges.

"Do you see all of those villages on the ridges to the east?"

"Yes," I replied.

"Do you see all the villages to the south?"

"Yes."

"They are all mine. They were my father's before me. If I want to send all the people of all those villages to war, I will send them."

"You will, will you?" I asked, straightening my own anatomy to full height. "Well, Njiri, if you will not listen to my words, you will have to feel the power of my pen. I go to write a letter to the D. C."

"*Bibi, Bibi,* what do you want?" called Njiri as I turned to retrace my steps to the mission.

"I want your subchiefs to go to Fort Hall to get Kamati and return him to school."

"*Nigwo, nigwo, tiga kurakara* [so be it, so be it, do not be angry]," he agreed.

But it was too late to rescue Kamati. He had been sent to German East Africa. As my boy and I rode into the mission station at sunset one day soon after this affair, we found it quiet and deserted. Not a soul was to be seen anywhere. Whatever had happened! Where could *Bibi* Collins and the boys have gone? It was almost dark before we saw them coming, and then she had a long tale of woe to relate.

"Mr. Lawford, the D. C. from Fort Hall, is in camp near the village of Njiri. This morning he sent his *askari* [soldiers] to Gathukiini outschool with orders to bring all of our people to his camp. The chiefs have told him all the young men of the district have enrolled in mission schools to avoid going to war. They also told him our people will not do their quota of work on the roads. The *askari* raided the villages of all our outschool people there, broke the clay pots of the women as they were cooking their corn and beans, beat the men and women and children into line, and drove them into the D. C.'s camp. Will you go and explain the true situation to Mr. Lawford?"

Early the next morning, walking up the path in the direction of the D. C.'s camp, I felt that I understood Queen Esther's frame of mind as she stood in the inner court of King Ahasuerus. Mr. Lawford was just and fair, but he was a strict disciplinarian. Unless he could be convinced of the true situation, he might close all the outschools, and the missionaries might have to leave the district in disgrace. However, he received me cordially at his tent door.

"I only wanted to get down to the bottom of the situation," he said after listening to an explanation of the background of the trouble. He was disturbed by the agitation among the subchiefs in Njiri's district, and he had come out here to camp determined to ferret out the cause of their accusations. "I have told the *askari* to bring all the mission people to me without violence, I want to talk to them."

"I fear the *askari* do not always remember their orders by the time they reach the villages," I suggested.

The interview had been encouraging, but it might be well for Mr. Lawford to have a little more enlightenment. Knowing the British devotion to a cherished social custom, I saw an opportunity to furnish that enlightenment.

"Thank you very much for listening to my story," I said to the D. C. as I rose to leave. "Would you come to the mission for a cup of tea at four today?"

"I will be pleased to come," he said.

From the mission a messenger was dispatched quickly to Gathukiini to tell Warimwe to bring to the mission by four o'clock the people whose backs bore the marks of violence.

"We had an agreement with your predecessor," I said to our guest as I poured the tea, "that the young men of the district who do not attend school will be drafted for porterage first, and that as needed the schoolboys will go in the order of their enrollment, the first to go last."

"That is true," said Mr. Lawford. "We have adhered strictly to this order."

"Furthermore, we have never failed to send the schoolboys to do road work when they have been ordered to do so. I fear the chiefs have misrepresented the whole affair."

"They are perfectly capable of doing that," he laughed over his teacup. "But who are all those people gathering down there by the school building?"

"They must be some of the people from the outschools," I answered with studied casualness. "Will you speak a word with them?"

When we had finished our tea, we rose and walked toward the school. Several of the D. C.'s *askari* who had come with him followed us.

"These are some of the people whose villages were raided when they were taken by violence to your camp," I explained when we came close to them.

"How could they be taken by violence? I ordered the *askari* to bring them in quietly using no force," said the D. C. in an annoyed tone of voice.

"Come, Kanyeri," I called, beckoning to an old man in the crowd. "Pull your blanket forward and show the *Bwana* your back."

Mr. Lawford gasped with astonishment as he gazed upon the cuts and bruises that covered the old man's back.

"Who did that?" he demanded of Kanyeri.

"That one," said the old man, pointing to one of the *askari* who had followed us.

Mr. Lawford walked up to the *askari,* took from him his sword and badges of Government authority, and ordered him to be placed with the prisoners who were being taken to Fort Hall to be tried in court.

"I will look into this matter thoroughly with Njiri and the subchiefs tomorrow," he promised.

It was easy to see the plots of the powers of darkness taking form. Deceitful chiefs and bribed interpreters would be used to black out the light and bring thick clouds of darkness to settle down upon the ridges. As these thoughts flashed through my mind, I addressed Mr. Lawford again.

"Would it be possible to hear this case at the mission, that we may hear the arguments put forth?"

"We do not usually do it," he said, "but as this is a mission case, I will hear it at the mission tomorrow morning at nine o'clock."

We spent the evening with the teachers preparing a long list of names of young men and elders of the district who never were known to be interested in school or mission affairs. Promptly at nine o'clock the next morning a long line of subchiefs, members of tribal councils, and Kikuyu elders, led by Njiri, marched down the path leading to the mission in all of their heathen splendor. They were bedecked with ornaments, feather headgears, and fur robes. Their faces, bodies, and hair glistened with a generous application of castor oil and red ocher. Conquering and to conquer, they pranced up to the mission to take their seats in court. Members of the four out-schools had been marshaled into line with their teachers and stood on the sidelines. Mr. Lawford was seated at a table. The two missionary *Bibis* occupied nearby chairs.

"Now," began the D. C. in Swahili, addressing all who were present and pausing at intervals for the Government interpreter to put his words into Kikuyu, "we are all working together to help the Agikuyu of this district to progress. The Government and the mission have joined forces to help the Kikuyu tribe learn how to take their place among the enlightened people of the world. If you should hitch two bullocks to a cart, one to pull forward and one to pull backward, what would happen?"

"Oh," replied the dignitaries, "the cart would not move forward."

"Just so, the Government and the mission are like two bullocks hitched to a cart. We are pulling together to help your cart to go forward. Njiri, you tell me all the people of your district have joined the mission. You say the young men are all enrolled in the schools and refuse your orders."

At this point I handed Mr. Lawford the prepared list of names.

"Will you ask Njiri, please, if he knows these men?" I requested.

"Kamau the son of Waweru," he read as he took the paper. "Do you know him, Njiri?"

"Yes."

"Does he live in your district?"

"Yes."

"Does he go to school?"

"No."

"Muciri son of Mbogo—do you know him?"

"Yes."

"Does he live in your district?"

"Yes."

"Does he go to school?"

"No."

Having asked the same questions regarding the first five names on the list and receiving the same answers, the D. C. dropped the paper. Fastening his black eyes, flashing with anger, upon Njiri and his subchiefs, he scorched them with words such as only he could utter. They looked to the east and to the west. The perspiration came out upon their foreheads, formed drops, and coalesced to make rivulets which forced their way through the layers of red paint. Their feather headgears drooped. They looked as if they wished for the earth to open up and hide them from the presence of him who had caught them in their own trap. That day Kinyona stood still and saw the salvation of the Lord.

Chapter 18

KAMBOGO'S "WELCOME"

"TWO MORE WEEKS and another term of school will close," remarked *Bibi* Collins one night as we were having our evening meal. "What shall we do during the holiday month?"

"Two of the Kikuyu schoolboys from a district below Marira want us to take a safari with them to their home villages."

Three weeks later the *Bibis* looked from their tent door over the beautiful banana-clothed ridges and valleys of Marira district, which was a part of our Githumu station territory. Our days were spent with the evangelist-teachers tramping over the ridges to villages and gardens to greet the people. During the evenings, we gathered the people around bonfires built in their villages where we explained to them the words of God and taught them to sing the songs of God.

"We cannot remember these words if we hear them once," they said. "Send us someone to tell us these words many times until we can remember them."

"Would you build a house for the meeting place?" asked one of the evangelists.

"*He, eeni* [why, yes], to build is not hard," they replied.

The landowner father of one of the boys went with Mucai, Kihoga, and the schoolboys the morning after this to measure off the plot he had volunteered to give for the school. A willing band of local men and boys soon gathered on the site to prepare it and were busy chattering and bantering each other in rivalry. The next day some of the porters, with local men to lead the way and help, were sent to cut poles for the framework. They were planting the first poles in the holes the local people had dug when two African tribal retainers employed by Government to carry Government orders and messages to all parts of the tribe appeared on the scene.

"We are sent," they said, "to bring to Fort Hall the sons of a landowner building a building here without the chief's permission."

There was nothing we could do. The two Kinyona schoolboys were led away to Fort Hall by the retainers. The village helpers hurried to their villages. The remaining members of the Kinyona safari returned to their camp for consultation.

"Is this not the work of Chief Kambogo?" began Mucai with a flash of fire in his eyes. "I have heard he has said there will never be an affair of school or the white man's God in his district while he is able to breathe."

"The subchief here is favorable toward the landowner giving this plot for a school," said another, "but Kambogo, the big chief over all, has gone to accuse us to the D. C. with many lies. He is a servant of *Cetani. No hatiri undu* [but it does not matter]. The God who commands us is stronger than all."

"Let us leave now the affair of this building and go down the ridges to give the people there the words of God," suggested Kihoga. "We will return to this place to finish our work later. The affair of Fort Hall will blow away. *Kai,* are they able to prevent the people here from learning to read the words of God? I say, No!"

"But we will still be in Kambogo's area," said the *Bibis.*

"*Kai,* who fears him!" retorted Mucai with a smile. "Let us go."

In the late afternoon our camp was set up on a hilltop to the northwest of Kambogo's own large, formidable village. In the morning Mucai and Kihoga, followed by the two *Bibis,* deliberately made their way through the village of wives' huts to the large *thingira* [the men's special hut], outside of which Kambogo sat on a low Kikuyu stool in the midst of his elders sunning himself. He took little notice of the approaching group.

"We have come to greet you," said Mucai, who was in the lead, offering his hand for the usual Kikuyu greeting.

"Um-m," grunted Kambogo, slowly extending his own hand.

"And these *Bibis* have come to greet you, too," Mucai went on as we moved forward in line to greet the chief.

When my turn came, Kambogo merely touched the tips of my fingers the way he might have touched some very despised thing.

"*Ni atia* [what is it]?" he asked coldly.

"Only greetings," I answered, retreating, "and we wish to greet the people of the villages."

"Um-m-m," he grunted again, by which he meant, "I am not on friendly terms."

The village people here were not as friendly either as those whom we had just left, but they were willing to sell us chickens, bananas, and food for the porters. On a small plain below Kambogo's village we found people living in villages built among banana groves and gardens. The soil was fertile, the food plentiful, but the people were lackadaisical due to malaria, yaws, syphilis, and other debilitating diseases.

"I have heard of this place," said Mucai. "It is called Muthithi."

"The people living all about this lower region of Kikuyuland are unlike the Agikuyu up where we live near the forest," added Kihoga. "They are despised by our people because of their bad diseases and lazy ways, but, *tiitheru* [of a truth], they grow much food and of a kind we are not able to grow."

All of us were tired in the evening of our day in Kambogo's locality, so we were glad to get back to camp and sit down to our evening meal of chicken stew. As soon as I had eaten, I turned in for the night, while the Africans chatted about their fire. I was alone, for *Bibi* Collins had had to go back to Kinyona. The bloodcurdling howls of hyenas had been heard since sundown. They were meandering up and down the ridges and around the nearby villages in search of victims. Suddenly the terrifying cry of one of these despised beasts just opposite the campfire sent the porters dashing off to their tents as though they had been shot. As he fled, Kihoga picked up a rock and sent it flying in the direction from which the howl had come. There was a swish through the bushes, and then silence brooded over the camp.

In the wee small hours of the morning, I was awakened by the crunching of chicken bones almost beside me, and I could hear the deep breathing of a beast. A hyena had ventured under the fly of the tent. There was but one fold of canvas between it and the camp cot.

"*Anake aya* [you young men, you]!" I shouted.

Immediately the war cry arose from the boys' tent. In a moment all of them were shouting and armed with Kikuyu weapons—knob sticks, spears, and clubs. Away into the darkness of the bushes they dashed in pursuit of the bold creature.

"*Kai, tiitheru* [of a truth]," they cried, "these have no shame or fear."

Nothing ever could be allowed to touch or molest the *Bibi* except it did so over the loyal dead bodies of these boys. Such was the character of Kikuyu boys and village porters in the pioneer days.

The two schoolboys who had been taken to Fort Hall did not

appear until after we got back to our station. They had been kept in jail until their case was heard. But when they had explained their side of the story to the D. C., apparently he had seen that the affair was a frame up and had sent the boys home.

After another school term had passed into history, an outschool was being built near the plain at Muthithi, the disease-ridden section of Chief Kambogo's district. The Githumu superintendent wanted a strong leader to launch the work. By this time Mucai's school at Mathanjiini shone like a beaconlight in the surrounding darkness of Kinyona, and he had married a staunch Christian girl, Naomi Wangari. He loved the people and the school, but the opposition to the light of the Gospel in Kambogo's district so challenged him that he responded gladly when asked to go to Muthithi, with its unpromising outlook. Turning his old school over to another teacher, he went forth with his wife, Naomi, and his sister, Nyambura.

A new missionary couple was sent to take over the work at Kinyona at this time, and my first furlough was due. Our faithful porter, Kihugu, had been brought in to the mission station with an attack of quinsy. The morning of my departure, I went out to his bed in the crude dispensary to bid him farewell—a final farewell this side of Heaven, for two weeks later the spirit of faithful Kihugu left his pain-wracked body.

"Go to your people far over the seas," were his last words to me. "Greet your father, your mother, your brothers, sisters, and all of your friends. When you have greeted them, tell them to allow you to return to Kikuyuland to tell the Kikuyu people about the words of God. *Thie na uhoro* [go in peace]."

KIJABE I
1919, 1920

Chapter 19

PATIENTS AND PATIENCE

THE FIRST WORLD WAR was over and for six months after returning to Kikuyuland from furlough, I had filled in at the Kijabe refuge home for persecuted girls who had broken away from heathenism. Then the field director called me into his office and told me that our splendid Canadian nurse was in a serious condition physically and must go home at once.

"We could call a worker from Matara for the girls," he said, "if you would take charge of Kijabe hospital."

"If I may be allowed to train Kikuyu boys and girls as assistants, I will try to fill in the gap," I told him, after taking time to think the matter through.

"I think they are too crude to take such training yet," he replied, "but if you want to try it, you have my blessing. You know the Kikuyu attitude toward the sick, though, and they are afraid of the spirits of the dead."

As a result of his permission, a call for hospital volunteers went out to Matara, Kinyona, Kijabe, and Githumu. On the appointed day twelve boys and two girls put in their appearance, among them Wambui and Kibura from the Kijabe girls' home.

Wambui had lived at the home for several years and had

taken to heart much of the teaching of the words of God. She was the one girl in this district who had refused to undergo circumcision. In fact, there were only three or four girls in all Kikuyuland at that time who had refused this operation. Wambui was being ridiculed and told that no Kikuyu would marry her, or if one should agree to do so, she never would bear children, but she was firm in her decision. The experience she was about to have in the hospital would strengthen her position greatly, for she would see for herself why, as a result of this mutilation, so many Kikuyu women died when unable to give birth to their first-born unless professional help was near.

Few of the fourteen volunteers were long out of paganism. Some were dressed in several yards of muslin, some in rags and tags, one in a castoff ladies' coat; but they were ready for the next step. This was the raw material out of which we were to fashion a hospital staff. Khaki uniforms were forthcoming in a short time, and it was a proud moment when they donned them. Faithful Kihoga, who had filled in at Kinyona as the first teacher of Mununga outschool, now was pressed into service as head dispensary boy, and we set about getting ourselves into working order. It was not long before we had occasion to test the metal of our new "staff."

"The Agikuyu have carried a sick *muthee* [old man] into Kijabe that he may be fixed," reported one of the new hospital assistants. "They are sitting on the grass by the outwards. Shall I tell them to take him home? He is very sick, near to die. Will we not have to bury him if he dies here?"

Aca, aca [no, no]!" I exclaimed. "This hospital was built to help sick people get well. We will come to see what we can do for him."

The new recruit was told to bathe the old man in warm water, give him a clean blanket, and put him in bed. His poor old legs were bent and stiff, his fever high, and his chest filled with many noises. He constantly muttered to himself. The following day he was calling for his wife, who had been dead for some years.

"*Kai,* what kind of thoughts does the *Bibi* think to give those Agikuyu permission to bring their dying old man here? They only want him to die here so we will be told to bury him. *Kai,* are the Agikuyu not wise and are the *athungu* [white people] not fools to be deceived by them!" exploded the indignant recruits outside the old man's ward.

The next day the old man's breathing was uneven. Now and again he called out in a dry whisper. Finally he closed his eyes and lay motionless.

"Who is going to bury the dead?" asked the new recruits as they lined up on strike before their *Bibi,* leaning on the shovels and Kikuyu hoes that Kihoga had given them with which to dig the grave.

"You know, *Bibi,* they bring their dead here to die so we will have to bury them. If they died in the village, the relatives would have to pay sheep and goats to those who buried them. We want you to tell them to pay us for burying the dead. That will end the affair of bringing people sick unto death to the hospital."

"Oh, but hospitals are built to give very sick people the best of care. We are here to help them and to tell them the way to a village where there is no sickness, and if they die here, we must be kind and helpful to the relatives so they will see there is a difference between Christian and heathen boys. Do you want the people to think you are heathen boys?"

"Come, let us go," said Gathitu, of Kinyona, picking up his shovel and starting off in the direction of the burying ground. One by one the others followed him.

"So you have come to the hospital to work?" called a very pleasant voice from the veranda of the dispensary.

"Oh, Johana, I am glad to see you. Where have you come from?"

"From Komothai to get some medicine for the baby. She is very sick. You remember Mary who was born at Matara? Keige has another baby now. Her name is Sarah. She is very sick in her chest."

It was good to look into Johana's honest face again, even though it was trouble that had brought him to Kijabe. He and Keige had walked on steadfastly in the path of God as they had been doing in the days of our first acquaintance at Matara. He was still the same Johana, a little older, more mature in his knowledge of the affair of God.

"How are you getting on with your school?" I asked him as I prepared the medicine for his baby.

"Very well. We have a good number in the bush school. The mothers and fathers try to prevent them, but they have a hunger to learn to read. Some are confessing their belief in *Jesu* and are in my class to teach them the Christian way. We hope to have a baptism at Komothai one day if God helps us. My father and mother now listen to the words of God, but they say they are following the Kikuyu God. I see Kihoga and Wanjiru, with little Virginia and James, have come to live at the hospital."

"Yes, Kihoga is the head dispensary boy."

"Who are those Kinyona boys in the kitchen?"

"The cook is Mwenja. He was employed as a cook for Lord Delamere in Nairobi, but he learned to read while he was on holiday at Kinyona and became a believer. He never returned to his work in Nairobi. He looks after me very well. I have no worries about the kitchen. The other boy is Joseph Muthungu. He wants to go to school at Kijabe, so I have taken him on to help him pay his expenses."

It was Mwenja who had brought to the kitchen this young lad who had dared to defy the custom of his tribe by refusing its all-important initiation rites and to receive circumcision from a mission doctor.

"Well, *Bibi,*" said Johana after I had given him instructions for the treatment of baby Sarah. "Abide in peace and the blessing of God. I must hurry home with the medicine."

It was time for the afternoon hospital rounds. A Kikuyu woman in heathen garb with a baby on her back sat on the dispensary bench.

"Are you with peace, and what is your trouble?" I asked as I passed by.

"That is for you to find out," snapped the woman.

"Where have you come from?"

"From wandering about Kikuyuland. I have come to the hospital to be cured of my sickness."

"Where are you sick?"

"In my body and in my head."

"Kihoga," I called, "find a bed for this woman. We will examine her tomorrow."

"What is your name?" questioned Kihoga, standing before her, register in hand.

"My name is Mwari *wa* Riua, daughter of the sun."

"That is a strange name," exclaimed Kihoga as he wrote it in the book. "I never heard of a Kikuyu woman called by such a name."

"Young man, you haven't heard all the things about Kikuyuland," she replied tartly. "You are too young to know the meaning of my name."

"*Bibi,*" cried the women patients with one accord when I went into their ward the next morning. "Why did you put this *mundu wa ngoma* [this person with evil spirits] in our house? Have we closed an eye all night? No! She has sung loud songs all the hours of the night. How can we get well of our sickness if we cannot sleep?"

Mwari *wa* Riua sat on the edge of her bed limp and exhausted.

"Why did you sing in a room where sick women want to sleep?" I asked her.

"Do not bite me with words. I could not help it. Rubutu came last night with all of his soldiers. First he came into my body and said he wanted to sing with my voice. I told him I was tired and wanted to rest. They refused to go. They left as the birds began to chirp. Did they come up to see you?" she asked in an uncanny voice. "They said they were coming to you when they left here."

"No," I replied firmly. "The Lord *Jesu* lives in my heart. He has overcome them. They fear Him."

"What is the meaning of Rubutu?" I asked Kihoga when he came into the dispensary.

"Oh, that means very many," he replied.

"In other words, Legion," I mused.

Sometimes as we went about our work, Kihoga and I talked of our old Matara friends.

"We have just had a letter from Wambui," he said one day as we walked toward the outwards, "the Wambui who went with you to the villages at Matara."

"Oh, yes, she went with Miss Alta to open work in the Belgian Congo."

"She is married now to Mwangi, *Bwana* Hurlburt's cook," continued Kihoga. "She says the work of learning the language of the people is very hard, but they are happy in the Lord. They ask us all to pray for them. Have you heard that Paul and Njeri are not happy because Njeri has no child? They have left the outschool we opened at Matara and have gone to live on a settler's farm upcountry as squatters."

"What kind of work do they do there?"

"Do the *athungu* [the white people] not tell them to build a hut on their land? And do they not give them land to cultivate? The *athungu* are wise in the ways they trap the Agikuyu. When they want bush land cleared for their farms, do they not measure off a large portion and give it to their squatters for their gardens? The land is rich. They quickly clear it up and plant their foods. They think they have found *munyaka* [good luck]. The potatoes grow very large. The peas and maize bring forth much food.

"*Ha, aca* [but, no], their luck is not so good. After a few seasons, the white man will take that for his field and give the Mugikuyu other land to clear for his gardens. And the affair of work! Every squatter must promise to give the farmer so many days of work every month. The white farmer may drive away a squatter any day—as for me, I do not think it is a good affair."

The women around the station had developed considerable confidence through the years in the medicines which the missionaries dispensed. They made frequent visits to us with all manner of complaints, but they did not see through all of our strange ways to treat them.

"No, no," wailed Wanjeri, the wife of Karanja who carried the mail from Kijabe railroad post office three miles up the hill to the mission. "No, I am afraid to take the medicine to put me to sleep."

"Very well," I told her, "then you will have to return to your home. I can do nothing for you."

Wanjeri started on her way but stopped to grumble to a group of women outside the dispensary door. She had lived three years of childless married life. She had come to ask the *Bibi* that she might fix her so she would give birth to a child. Why could the *Bibi* not give her medicine to drink? Why did she tell her she must go to sleep on a table? How would she know it was a good affair if she were asleep? She persisted in her belief that there was some other way out of the difficulty and was back again before many days.

"Well, Wanjeri, what do you want today?" I asked her. "Are you ready to lie down on the table and go to sleep?"

"No," she replied sullenly. "I want some medicine in a bottle to fix my stomach."

"I told you there is no help for you unless you are willing to do what we tell you to do."

Turning on her heel, Wanjeri went down the path in a pout, but she was in a different frame of mind the next time she put in her appearance at the dispensary.

"I have come to the hospital to take the medicine which will put me to sleep," she announced humbly as she stood first on one foot and then the other, looked down at the floor, and drew long breaths.

"Now we will be able to help you," I said cheerfully, "and you will see we have been telling you the truth. Before long you will be coming into the hospital to give birth to your child."

A faint smile flitted over the features of Wanjeri as she looked up into the *Bibi's* face. Arrangements were made for her slight operation in a few days. A year and a half of busy days went by at the hospital after that, and a new doctor and his wife, who was a clever nurse, were in charge of the hospital when Wanjeri was admitted again. When her baby boy arrived safely, the news traveled far and wide.

"Where did all these women patients come from and what is their trouble?" asked a visitor at the hospital a short time later.

"Oh, these are childless women," the visitor was told. "They have come from all part of Kikuyuland. They have heard about Wanjeri. A rumor has gone abroad that if you want to give birth to a child, you go to Kijabe Hospital."

With the coming of the new doctor and his wife, the Kijabe hospital needs were taken care of, but another ailing medical work needed to be revived. Some time previous to this, the doctor at Githumu had left his pioneer work to go on furlough. To reopen that was my next assignment. Knowing that the housing facilities at the new station were meager for the accommodation of another worker, I packed and stored my goods at Kijabe and prepared to journey to Githumu with my camp cot, a blanket bag, a box of clothing suitable for pioneer work, some epsom salts, antiseptics, a few simple instruments, my mule, and the kitchen boy, Muthungu.

"I want permission to leave the hospital work," announced Kibura at the close of a day's duties just before I left for Githumu.

"Will you not remain to help the *Bibi* who has just arrived?"

"I should like to remain, but Mwangi, who has paid sheep and goats to my father, tells me I am to marry him now. A boy from Matara has come to ask Wambui if he may pay sheep and goats to her father also."

"This is the way of girls," I laughed, "but if you both remember all the things you have learned in the hospital and teach your children about them, your training here will not be fruitless."

Thus one of the dire predictions made by Wambui's friends and relatives when she had refused the initiation rites had come to naught. The other was to be proved false as well, for eventually Wambui became the mother of six healthy children—another conclusive demonstration of the power of light over darkness.

GITHUMU I

1921, 1922

Chapter 20

A PIONEER MEDICAL WORK

IT WAS THREE O'CLOCK on a sunny afternoon when I alighted from Ndeithia's back near the two banana-leaf thatched shacks at Githumu that were the present home of the McKenrick family. Ndeithia began to nibble the tender grass about her, and Muthungu sat down in the shade of a nearby wattle tree. The McKenricks came down the path to welcome the new member of their staff. The *Bibi* McKenrick had inherited the dispensary work after the departure of the doctor for furlough but, having a small, rather delicate baby, had had to leave the work for the most part to an untrained African boy.

"I am sorry I have no supplies to turn over to you," said the *Bibi* the next morning as I started out for the dispensary. "I have nothing but a bill for some medicines which have been used already—but I have decided not to present it."

"Thank you, I am grateful for small favors," I laughed.

The dispensary was a rough building. The sides were made of poles and sticks thatched with banana leaves. The roof was thatched with grass which hung in dull, untidy lines around the edges. To give sleeping quarters to inpatients, a large, one-room building of the same materials was being constructed. I stepped across the path to inspect the unfinished building and peered through the doorway. From the floor, like vicious evil spirits, a cloud of fleas arose to attack me. I fled in distress to recover and reclothe myself; then went to report the situation to the wife of the senior missionary.

"We will soon deal with the fleas," *Bibi* Raynor promised calmly. "I will send Cira down in the morning."

Cira appeared the next morning prepared to administer the flea cure. She journeyed alternately to the river for water and to the cowpen for dung. These she mixed with her bare feet in the middle of the dirt floor of the new building. Next she slithered a quantity of it with her feet to a far corner of the room, shoved another quantity to the opposite corner, and filled in the space between. The other half of the room received the same treatment. Then Cira announced, "The fleas are finished." Sure enough, the fleas had perished and were buried. The ammonia in the cow dung had been effective.

The next problem was beds for the patients. When the people heard that a missionary had arrived to give them medicine, they carried in their sick and laid them in the grass outside the dispensary. Night came on. It might rain. Where were they to sleep? Small, temporary tumble-down buildings stood about here and there. They were requisitioned for the immediate need. Bundles of dry banana leaves were placed on the earth floors. A fire was built in the middle of each floor. The patients were given a blanket and made as comfortable as possible, but if it rained hard, down came the rain through the decayed grass roofs. It was imperative to finish the inpatient building as soon as possible.

Some willing workmen were found.

"Bring some crotched posts, some poles, and some thin, willowy sticks," were their first instructions.

"Plant a row of crotched posts along the long inside wall of the building," I directed when they had brought their materials. "Plant another row five feet from the wall. Do the same on the other side. That will leave a two-foot passage in the center."

The next step was to place the poles in the crotches and tie them securely with *ndigi,* the stout inner bark of a bush that was used for string. The thin sticks were arranged in neat rows across the poles and also tied with *ndigi.* Now the framework of two long beds was completed. Mattresses were improvised of brachen covered with mats made of the spongy ribs of banana leaves. In the course of ten days, the building and beds were completed.

The men patients were assigned to the long beds on one side, the women to the other. In a few weeks the beds were filled. The sick were packed literally like sardines in a tin—yaws, flu, syphilis, leprosy, tick fever—all together. There was nothing else to do. There never were sufficient blankets to supply each patient with one. I spread out what we had over the rows of patients.

"*Ni wega, ni wega* [it is so good, so good]," they said as they ducked their heads under the blankets. Probably they never had slept in such a comfortable bed before in their lives.

The news of the inpatient building spread rapidly throughout Githumu district from the forest to the plains. The sick who could would come on foot. Others were carried in by relatives. Many came to buy medicine for sick relatives in their villages. It was impossible to carry on with just one untrained medical boy. To my joy, Muirigi turned up to greet me one morning—Muirigi who had been one of the Githumu volunteers for medical training at Kijabe. He was back in his own district and interested in obtaining work.

"Are you with peace, Muirigi?" I greeted. "*Tütheru* [of a truth], I greatly rejoice to see you. Are you looking for hospital work?"

"I will not refuse to work in a hospital," he replied smiling.

"I want two boys. Do you know of any other boy who would be willing to come with you?"

"A boy named Keiru has said he would do the work of helping the sick."

"Bring him with you and come tomorrow morning prepared to live at Githumu and go to work."

"*Nitugoka* [we will come]."

"I have engaged two hospital boys," I told *Bibi* Raynor in the afternoon, "but now I want two girls to help with the women. Have you any suggestions?"

"Cira seems to be intrigued with the hospital. Perhaps she would help you," she suggested. "And I will ask Mucai to send Nyambura. She is such a wonderful little Christian. They say she wins many of the heathen women at Muthithi outschool by asking them to allow her to help them carry their babies and do their work."

"Let me see, Nyambura is now thirteen or fourteen years of age—rather young—but mature for her years, and she has not been brought up in a heathen home. There are many things she can do in the treatment of children and women. Let us give her a try."

Our African hospital staff was now complete—two boys and two girls. Morning by morning as I moved down the aisle between the men and women directing the assistants in the care of the various and sundry African diseases, I wondered whatever the medical world, or even the missionary-minded Christian people, in the homeland would think if they could look upon this scene. They would be shocked, surely. I was shocked, too, by what I saw. On the other hand, these were better quarters than the same people would have had in their villages. They were warm and dry, and grateful to be taken into the hospital and given kind attention.

After all, I wondered, what would the medical world or the Christian people at home have done in such an emergency as I had faced when sent to carry on a pioneer medical work in the depths of Kikuyuland with no funds on hand. One course might have been to have taken a look at the discouraging situation and written a letter to the field council to remind them that no one ever had been trained to do medical work under such conditions, or that unless better buildings and equipment were supplied, one would look for other fields in which to work. Another course would have been to have gotten busy with other work in the district—of which there was aplenty—and to have neglected the medical work. In such an event, what would have happened to the multitudes of sick and dying in Githumu district with none to have compassion on them, and no one willing to minister to the bodies of those for whom Christ had died?

So we went on, making the most of what we had, charging a fee within the means of Agikuyu patients to pay for our medicines, daily seeking by means of the Gospel light to drive out the darkness in the hearts of those who came to us with physical diseases—and the Lord stood by and blessed us. No one ever was turned away for lack of money to pay the fee, yet at the end of two years, when the doctor returned, we were able to turn over the hospital work to him with a balance on hand of one thousand rupees to pay for more supplies.

Chapter 21

THE HABITATIONS OF CRUELTY

IT WAS A THURSDAY EVENING, the time when the Githumu mission boys and girls who had believed the good news of salvation went to the villages to encourage others to believe on the great Saviour they had found. A group of us had entered Nyanjui's village and received a friendly welcome there.

"Are all the people here?" asked the mission boys of the men, as men, women, boys, girls, and children came from all directions to squat around the fire built in the middle of the village.

"Yes. Sing us the songs of God," said the owner of the village.

"Are all the women here?" I asked.

"All but one, and she is not able to come."

"But why not?"

"Oh, she is sick."

"You must take me to see her before we sing."

"She is a worthless person. Sing us the songs of God," they said impatiently.

"We will not sing until I see the sick woman," I insisted.

Snatching a firebrand from the fire to light his way, one

of the men led me down a bushy, winding path to the back of the village. Stopping by a hut, we entered the low doorway. The hut was dark except for a few dying embers in the middle of the hard dirt floor. The man laid some dry splinters on the coals and blew up a blaze. In the flickering shadows, I saw the emaciated body of a woman lying on the floor near the fire. Her six-weeks'-old baby, a tiny bundle of skin and bones, was tugging at her dry breast. They had been left to die together.

"Tomorrow she must come to Githumu," I told the man before we went back to the gathering around the fire.

"Take the stretcher out to Nyanjui's village," the hospital boys were ordered the next morning. "Bring the sick woman and her baby to the hospital."

"We have bathed the mother and baby and put them in bed. The woman has a very bad sickness. The baby might live if we give her food," reported Cira at noon.

The mother was found to have an advanced dropsical condition due to an incurable disease. The girls explained to her in clear Kikuyu the love of the Saviour for her, and the way to receive Him and trust in His cleansing blood. At the end of the month she was buried in a plot that was reserved for the burial of hospital patients.

With food and care, the baby, Nyakiega, flourished and grew rapidly. She was a great favorite because of her laugh and play when she was transferred from the hospital to live with the small orphan children in the girls' home. Later she was adopted by a Christian woman living at Mathanjiini outschool.

An urgent call came in from a distant village. A Kikuyu woman had been in labor for days.

"Come and help her," pleaded the messenger.

The need was urgent. I mounted Ndeithia and followed the messenger. Nyambura came on behind with the maternity kit. We traveled for an hour and a half over the narrow, winding path to the village. There the exhausted woman, supported by an old Kikuyu midwife, reclined on leaves on the hut floor.

"We cannot see to work here," I said to Nyambura after sizing up the situation. "Cut some green banana leaves from that nearby grove. Spread them under the shade of the tree near the hut. We will carry her out to the light. It is a difficult, complicated case. The baby is dead, but we will try to save the life of the mother."

Nyambura made haste to obey orders. We laid the woman on the banana leaves under the tree and set to work.

"You give her the anesthetic," I directed, "and you can help me also if delivery is possible."

When hope was almost abandoned, I stood up to relieve the cramps in my back and relax my tired arms. Looking out over the bushes in the direction of the homeland, my spirit cried out within me: "When will help come? When will doctors and nurses, fired by the love of Christ for the perishing womanhood of Africa, come to the rescue? Yet we never can hope for a sufficient number to come to meet the need. What then is the solution?"

Looking behind me, I saw Nyambura tenderly trying to soothe the now semiconscious woman with words of hope and comfort.

"There is the solution," flashed the answer to my question, "trained African girls. I may spend my years and strength helping a few Kikuyu women. When my years are spent, the work will cease. If I could train African girls, inspired by the love of Christ to do the work I am doing, I could multiply myself a hundredfold and the rescue work would continue. The Lord being my Helper, I will train African girls."

Had God brought me face to face with this trying experience to speak to me of His plan for my future work? I turned back to the suffering woman.

"We will have one more try," I said to Nyambura, bracing myself for a final effort.

The dead child was brought forth, the mother revived and put to rest in her hut. She had passed through a needless ordeal and had lost a child that might have lived had it not been for the ceremonial mutilations by which her tribe had heralded her entrance into womanhood.

"*Bibi! Bibi! Bibi!*" called a voice through the window in the gray dawn of a cold, misty morning. "Wanja, your Wanja, is sick."

"What is her sickness?"

"She is sick in her stomach."

Throwing something warm about me, I bade the man meet me at the dispensary. Thinking from his description that Wanja was suffering from a digestive disorder, I prepared a remedy, explained how the medicine was to be given, and promised to come to his village soon.

"When you come," said he as he turned reluctantly away, "bring your *magathi.*"

"What!" I exclaimed in sudden realization of the truth when he asked for the forceps. "Is Wanja not able to give birth to a child?"

Calling Cira, who was asleep in the dormitory, I gathered up a few supplies and returned to my room to dress.

"Oh, Cira," I gasped in dismay as we neared the village, "have they taken Wanja to the bush?"

"I see a group of women surrounding someone in the bush," replied Cira.

Sure enough, there lay Wanja, just as they had dropped her, with her face upturned, unconscious of the cold, drizzling rain. Kneeling down beside her in the dripping bushes, I saw at a glance that Wanja was one more victim to be sacrificed in Kikuyuland to the god of fertility on the altar of female circumcision. A simple clip of the surgical scissors here and there in time would have saved the life of Wanja and her first-born.

"Too late, too late," I sighed as the village people gathered about the tragic scene.

"Why did you wait till Wanja was dying to call me?" I reproved them.

"Do not scold us," they said. "We wanted to call you, but the witch doctor said, 'Sacrifice a red sheep, and Wanja will give birth.' We did so.

"The next day we wanted to call you, but he said, 'If you call her, Wanja and her baby will both die. Sacrifice a black goat.' We did so.

"The next day he said, 'If you call the *Bibi,* every woman in this village will die in childbirth. Sacrifice a white goat.' We did so.

"Last night he told us if we threw the strap, Wanja used to carry wood, over her hut she would give birth to her child. We did so. This morning we came for you. Do not scold us, *Bibi,* we were afraid to disobey the words of the witch doctor."

For answer I got down on my knees again and delivered the dead child to convince them of how simply the life of Wanja and her child might have been saved if they had called me in time. As I did so, Wanja took one more breath as her spirit departed Kikuyuland.

"How long, how long before the light breaks over these Kikuyu ridges to bring help, hope, and deliverance from the powers of darkness to Kikuyu womanhood?" I asked as Cira and I made our way through the wet, bushy path back to the mission station.

Four stalwart Kikuyu warriors marched down the path that led to the dispensary. They were perfect specimens of heathen Kikuyu. Their bodies and hair were adrip with castor oil and red clay. Each was clad in about two yards of unbleached muslin saturated with the oil and clay mixture. On their shoulders they carried a stretcher made of two poles with willowy sticks placed crosswise and fastened in position with native string.

A Kikuyu woman in a tattered goatskin garment lay on dry banana leaves on top of this stretcher.

The warriors dropped their burden, beckoned to the *Bibi* to come, and sat down in the grass. At a glance I saw that the woman had been ill for many weeks. The marks of suffering were all to evident. She was emaciated and semiconscious. She had never heard of the love of the Lord Jesus, or how He had given His life on Calvary's cross that she might have life and have it more abundantly. Now she was too weak and too ill to hear the story.

"How long has she been sick?" I asked the warriors.

"We cannot remember."

"Why did you not bring her to the hospital before it was too late?"

"Her owner told us to carry her in today."

"I fear you have waited too long, but we will do our best to help her."

A few days later the one who had sent her to the hospital, and was called her man, came to see this woman. When he found her lying on the bed beside the other women patients, he looked her over in much the same way that he would inspect a sick sheep or cow, and left the hospital without saying a word to anyone. Two days later he reappeared with his brother. Together at her bedside they discussed her condition and decided her fate.

"I do not think she will get well," said the man to his brother. "Already we have wasted many sheep and goats trying to appease the spirits which have brought this sickness upon her. If she dies here, they will tell us to bury her. To touch death will make us unclean. We will have to call the witch doctor, provide him with a fat sheep, and pay him a fee to remove our defilement. This wife never has borne me a living child. I will be able to reclaim from her father most of the sheep and goats I paid for her."

"Our best plan," said the brother, "is to take her to the bush and end the matter."

Standing nearby, I could hear their conversation.

"No, no, you may not take her to the bush," I protested.

"Have we not paid for her? Is she not our property?" snarled the man, seizing the patient's arm.

Before anyone could prevent them, the two men had pulled the woman from her bed and were dragging her down the aisle toward the door. In their hurry they jammed her shoulder against the doorpost. Writhing in pain, she looked up at me pleadingly, but there was nothing we could do to stop them. By custom and law she was their property. Sick and semiconscious though she was, she knew she was being taken to the bush.

Unmoved, the men hustled their property along the path, her heels leaving zigzag trails in the dust behind her. Down the hillside path back of the dispensary they went, never stopping until they reached the foot of the hill. Turning off the path, they dropped her under a clump of bushes, pulling her body well under the low-hanging branches. Then they built a fire at a little distance and sat down to watch a while before they deserted her.

Night came on, and I could not forget the patient in the bushes. Taking some nourishment and a stimulant, I made my way to the clump of bushes to make one last appeal to the men to bring the woman back to the hospital. They had made their decision, however, and were not to be moved by any appeal or reward.

All I could do was to turn away and wend my way back up the hill path in the direction of my abode. The darkness of the night enveloped me, and my thoughts were troubled within. A lump rose in my throat. The sense of men and women living on the ridges all about, whose eyes were blinded to the light of love and human kindness, stifled me. I could see the fires and hear the songs in a minor key rising from hundreds of villages on the surrounding hills and valleys. Uncounted numbers of men, women, and children were there. Their hearts had not been touched or illuminated by the love of God or the Light of the world. A cruel, ruthless power reigned over them. Like some monster, it barred the entrance of the light of truth, reason, kindness, shutting them in to live with darkness—and did not the psalm say that "the dark places of the earth are full of the habitations of cruelty"? But above the darkness of the night, the stars were shining.

"Though my efforts have failed and my patient lies in the darkness of the bushes, God sitteth on His throne above the stars. He sees and knows and cares," came the comforting thought.

Throwing the light of the lantern on the dark path ahead, I followed its light to my shack and retired. In the early hours of the morning, before daybreak, I was aroused by the loathsome howls of a hyena as he made his way up the ridge path in search of food. As I listened, I knew he had caught a scent. It was leading him to a clump of bushes just off a narrow path at the foot of the hill. A succession of hideous, brutal, triumphant cries echoed through the quiet morning air. I was well acquainted with the ghastly habits of this despised creature of the African bush. I knew he had craned his huge neck to reach beneath some low-hanging bushes. I thought I could see him snap his great fangs into the flesh of my patient and draw her out of her bushy bed. Was she dead? Did she know? Who would ever know! Lifting her in his big murderous jaws, he would crash through the bushes, bearing her to a path which led down the ridge to a noted place, a side hill filled with caves where the hyenas lived and reared their young.

"It is the village of the hyenas," the Africans would say as they shivered and passed it hurriedly on their way.

One could see, scattered about the mouths of the caves, bits of goatskin clothing, head ornaments, and odd fragments of human anatomy, the telltale remains of many a victim. I knew that when the hyena reached that place, the colony of hyenas, great and small, male and female, would rush from the mouths of those caves. Howling, snarling, fighting, they would battle free-for-all for a meal. One would seize an arm and run in one direction; others would snatch the legs and plunge in the opposite direction. I could visualize it all in the darkness of that early morning hour. The tragic end of my patient was the result of being born, growing to womanhood, and dying in a land ruled by the powers of darkness.

"He who commanded the light to shine out of darkness hath shined in my heart. He has given me the light of the knowledge of the glory of God in the grace of Jesus Christ. I will allow nothing to deter me from giving this light to these people," I vowed as the dim light of another day was beginning to dawn over the ridges.

There were other women at the hospital waiting to be ministered to. Others would be carried in that day. It was my glorious privilege to stand in their midst to bring to them some knowledge of the light that God had now commanded to shine upon a Kikuyu world.

Chapter 22

WARNING SIGNALS

"URI MUHORO [are you with peace]? And where have you come from?" I asked a bright-faced young man whom I met in the path on one of the early days at Githumu.

He was Paul Njuguna, the teacher-evangelist. Although he belonged to this district and had gone to school at Githumu, I had known him in Kinyona days, for he had joined forces with the young converts when they had carried the Light of the world into the dark places of Kikuyuland.

"I have come from the outschools *etherero* [down east]," he said, with his usual bright smile. "Today I have been giving the words of God to the Itara school. Do you remember the safari we took down to that place? Do you remember how the landowner gave us a plot and permission to build a school, and how, in the midst of our building, Kambogo accused us to the District Commissioner at Fort Hall? Ha, but God was on our side! Had we not gone to teach as He commanded us to do? *Cetani* could not overcome us. Warimwe, of Gathukiini, is teaching there now."

Well did I remember our troubles with Kambogo on that safari, and Warimwe's school at Gathukiini where the girls were snatched away by their parents for the circumcision rites, and the believers were beaten by the D. C.'s soldiers when the chiefs were plotting against our Kinyona schools.

"Did you know, *Bibi,*" Paul went on, "that as a result of our village meetings on the safari, seven Kikuyu girls, my sister among them, came to Githumu to have the holes in the lobes of their ears sewed up as a sign to their people that they had left the customs of Kikuyuland to walk in the path of God? We have an outschool at Githima, too, now. *Tiitheru* [of a truth], *Bibi,* the Gospel is the power of God unto salvation."

We talked of all the bush schools now built in Githumu district, for these were days when missionaries and African believers were being encouraged by the flourishing Gospel centers that had sprung up everywhere to send their beams of light over the ridges, and when they rejoiced over the many, even among the young aristocracy of Kikuyuland, who had stepped out of darkness to walk in the light of those beams. We spoke of Muhuthu, the herdboy of Matara who had been thrown into the Chania River for following the path of God, and how he had been sent to teach at Irera. We spoke of Mucai and Naomi, who had left the prosperous little school Mucai had opened at Mathanjiini for a difficult place in Githumu district.

"The opposition from Kambogo has been very strong," I said. "Disease abounds there, too, and Naomi has lost three babies. Did you hear how the schoolboys of Muthithi carried Mucai to Githumu hospital more dead than alive a short time ago? When I asked him if he did not want to be transferred to a healthier district, he said:

" 'No, we do not want *Cetani* to think he can drive us out of a place because of hard experience.' "

"God is working," agreed Paul thoughtfully. "Isaiah Mucina was one of the small herdboys that Mucai led to Christ at Mathanjiini. Now he has gone to build a school and teach at Ndogomano, near Kambogo's village."

We had reason to remember Ndogomano.

"Ha," laughed Paul, "was that not the place where the hyenas howled about our camp and one was near to walking into your tent? *Tüthberu* [of a truth] the wicked spirits of *Cetani* try to frighten the people of God when they go to carry the light to those who have never seen the light."

"But has not *Jesu* overcome these evil spirits of darkness?"

"He has done that, and in His strength we will carry the Light of the world to all the Kikuyu villages on the ridges," finished Paul in a triumphant note as he turned to take a path leading back to the battle front.

In January, 1922, the McKenricks were away for a short holiday and I was eating alone. Muthungu had cleared away the dishes from my evening meal, and was standing in the doorway of the room where I was writing.

"I want to talk with you," he said.

"Come in, then." I turned from my work.

"It is a very big affair," began Muthungu, holding his mouth with his hand in the characteristic Kikuyu gesture that signified astonishment. "The word being passed around is this: They say you missionaries have not come to Africa for a good purpose. They say that you pretend to be friends of the people, but in truth you are Government spies and live among us to learn all about our affairs. They say that when you and *Bwana* McKenrick go to the meetings of the missions in Nairobi, in truth you go to report Kikuyu affairs to Government. The people are told not to trust in the medicine the white people give them because they will be deceived."

"But surely you do not believe these words to be true," I protested, shocked at the suggestion.

"*Bibi,* perhaps these things are not true of the missionaries, but the white people who came to live in Kenya have taken land which belongs to the Kikuyu people. We are told that all the land of the Agikuyu live on and cultivate, the Government calls Crown land—that it does not really belong to the people. If we think this affair is not true, we are told to ask the Government to give us title deeds to our land, and then we will see them refuse to do this. Is this not an affair of stealing our land by trickery? Did not our forefathers buy from or treat or bargain with other tribes for the entire Kikuyu country? How can people come from other countries and say our land belongs to their government?"

"I know," I answered sympathetically, but aware also of how the present state of affairs had come about. "I know that the Kikuyu tribe has lost some of its tribal lands. I know how, before 1900, large areas were depopulated by famine and smallpox. The Government did not know your Kikuyu system of land tenure or that every foot of these areas had a legitimate owner who would claim the land eventually, and I know that between 1902 and 1907 the Government unwisely encouraged white settlers to develop coffee plantations on this temporarily abandoned land. But I hear that Britain now proposes to send a Royal Commission to Kenya to investigate the matter and try to bring about a satisfactory settlement.

"As to the missionaries being Government spies, our time at the meetings of the Alliance of Missions in Nairobi is spent in defending the rights of the Africans, pointing out injustices and seeking ways to have them corrected. We continually rereport cases of forced labor such as coffee planters sending recruiters of labor to the reserve to force Kikuyu to go to pick coffee, or the seizing of Kikuyu village girls by tribal retainers when they are sent out in the villages on Government business. You know we missionaries have not come to Kenya to buy land. You see we have only five acres for this mission station. It is very little for schools, dormitories for boys and girls, church, hospital, dwelling houses, and athletic fields. These five acres are being used only for the development and enlightenment of the Agikuyu."

"I see this to be true," admitted Muthungu, "but the loss of much valuable land around Nairobi rankles in the hearts of young Kikuyu men who want to build good houses and farm their land to make food money. Another affair the Agikuyu are angry about is the *kipandi.*"

The *kipandi* was a registration document giving the name of the bearer, his father's name, his village and district location, and his number. Employers were required to state on the *kipandi* the wage paid, date of employment, date of dismissal, and remarks on the character of the employee. A metal case was supplied with this document to protect it from weather, rats, and termites.

"We are compelled to carry our *kipandi* about with us the way a dog carries his tag," Muthungu continued hotly. "If we are on a journey, and a policeman appears and finds we are without our *kipandi,* he arrests us. All these things make the Kikuyu very suspicious about why the white men came to live in our land. The young Kikuyu men who have a desire to progress and stand for our tribal rights have formed a society called the Kikuyu Central Association. Many of them are the first in the tribe to learn the affair of reading. It is their intention to find a way to get back the lost land of the Agikuyu. Their leader is Harry Thuku. He has an office in Nairobi and a motorcar. He goes to all the African markets and to the squatters on the upcountry farms to unite them in an effort to get back our land. They say some of the leading Indians in Kenya are sympathetic and are helping the Agikuyu in this affair."

Muthungu had relieved his mind for the time being. It was late, and he had not cooked his evening meal.

"Good night, *Bibi,*" he said. "We have had a long talk."

For young men like Muthungu, who had taken their stand against the age-long spiritual, mental, and moral darkness with which the god of this world had enveloped Kikuyuland, there were new dangers in the political unrest about them. Having come to know the intellectual and material benefits which always accompany those who walk in the light of the Gospel, and being true children of their native tribe, their patriotism created burning desires within them for the progress of their people. Yet they were not sufficiently mature either in years or in the knowledge of God to discern the form of the prince of darkness when he masqueraded as an angel of light in a costume which was set off with many accessories of genuine value. Bright-minded mission boys, with their progressive attitude, were being made the object of subtle attack by subversive outside forces even then at work to infiltrate the aggressive Kikuyu tribe with a nationalism which would eventuate in widespread racial hatred and anti-Christian demonstration.

Harry Thuku was a youth who had professed conversion and received training in a neighboring evangelical mission. The cause which he represented had just grievances to which were added false insinuations concerning both Government and missions. During this period, the K. C. A. was gaining widespread support among the younger adults of the tribe who already were being alienated from the traditions of their fathers and in various degrees were taking on Western ways. The old tribal elders held tenaciously to the traditional Kikuyu way of life, with its taboos and palavers and sacrifices, but they were opposed to the K. C. A.

One evening several months after the talk with Muthungu, the boys in the kitchen were talking in excited, high-pitched voices. I called Muthungu to come to my room.

"What is the trouble?" I asked him.

"A Kamanyaka boy we know has just returned from Nairobi. There is a big affair there," he replied, greatly agitated. "The police officers arrested Harry Thuku and put him in the Nairobi jail. The Agikuyu in Nairobi were very angry. They gathered around the jail and said they would not leave until Harry was given back to them. They went around to the houses and made all the Agikuyu working for white people to leave their work and join the crowd. The Government officers asked the crowd many times to choose a committee to meet them and the governor to listen to their words, but the people only shouted more loudly for Harry. Finally the crowd marched on the jail to deliver him by force. The police shot into the crowd. Many were killed and wounded. Nikola, of Kamanyaka school, who lives just over the ridge, was there. His right leg was shot off."

Muthungu shuddered as he mentioned Nikola.

"It is a very bad affair," he went on. "They have taken Harry away from Nairobi. We do not know where he is. But you will see this is not the end of the affair. The K. C. A. say they will never rest until the Government agrees to return the land that has been taken from the Agikuyu and allows Harry to return to his home."

The Kikuyu teachers and older pupils at Githumu were greatly stirred up over this outbreak in Nairobi, and none more deeply than Muthungu. Other affairs also were occupying his mind during the weeks that succeeded the Harry Thuku riot, and he came to me one day for another serious talk.

"Bibi," he said, "I will finish the lessons of the Githumu school at the close of this term. Long ago, when I returned to our village from Nairobi, my brother Paul told me to make my choice in the affair of circumcision. *Tiitheru* [of a truth], it was a very big affair to decide. When I went out to the bushes alone to make my decision, I prayed the Lord to prevent me from beginning to walk in the Christian way if He saw that, along the way in time to come, I would desert that way to return to the path of darkness. When I went to the mission to be circumcised, I made my choice for a lifetime. Now I have come to tell you I want to continue my education that I may prepare to become a useful servant of the Lord to help the Agikuyu to leave their customs of sin and their desire to follow their old ways of life forever. I see other people of the world have much

knowledge of many affairs, while the Africans have been left far behind."

"I am glad to hear all you have told me," I said, "but I want to point out to you one stumbling block. Other young Kikuyu men are stirred with the same desire for progress and development. This is one of the natural fruits of the Gospel of good news which is being broadcast in Kikuyuland. But other forces are being released in this land. The god of this world is sending them abroad. Many, not being able to see the difference between the true and the false, will be deceived by them. Your only safeguard will be a dependence on the power of the Lord *Jesu* to walk with you and to keep you."

"My brother Waitara at Kijabe wants advanced school, too," added Muthungu.

"I will write to the principal of the Scotch Presbyterian Mission school at Kikuyu and ask him if he will admit you to this school at the beginning of the new year. Githae has finished here, too. I will ask if they will have a place in the dormitory for the three of you."

So it came about that when the doctor returned from furlough to take up the medical work at Githumu once more, and I went to take temporary charge of a joint-mission project for incorrigible women before going on my own furlough, Muthungu, his younger brother Waitara, and Githae left Githumu for further training. Mucai's sister Nyambura, who had been a great help to me in the hospital, was ready for advanced work and went also. What, I wondered, would be the fruit of these promising young lives in the years to come?

KIJABE II
1927-1937

Chapter 23

BRIGHT SKIES FOR THE GIRLS

THE YEARS OF LIVING in close touch with the tragedies surrounding the womanhood of Kikuyuland had caused me to search for a means of delivering women from the cruelties and bondage that imprisoned them, and I was led to see clearly that the training of Kikuyu Christian girls to minister to the women of their tribe was the only solution. The organization of the Kijabe Girls' Training School was the result.

Kijabe had offered asylum to Kikuyu girls ever since the turn of the century when Nyakeiru, the first Kikuyu girl to escape from her village, had fled to Alta Hurlburt for refuge on the mission station. The situation was the same on every Kikuyu station. Girls were being sheltered who came to escape the sorrows of forced marriages or because they wanted to walk in the path of God, which they never would have been allowed to do in their heathen villages.

For lack of workers, the Kijabe refuge home had been closed for more than a year before my return from furlough. At the beginning of 1927 with *Bibi* Irene Rezac to help me, we launched a new type of training school for Kikuyu girls. I had spent two years studying the various Negro schools of America's Southland to help in forming a sound policy for our school. We took over an old rambling pioneer brick structure infested by rats, fleas, and jiggers across a narrow deep ravine from the main part of Kijabe station, cleaned it up, and opened a training center for the many Kikuyu girls—some refugees, some daughters of Christian parents—now clamoring for admission.

Among the first to register was Miriam Wambui, a shy wee girl of about ten years, from Mathanjiini. Her father and mother were dead. According to Kikuyu law, she was the property of her brother, Isaiah Mucina, one of the herdboys who was taught to read at Mucai's outschool but now grown to be a staunch, progressive Christian young man. He felt keenly his responsibility for the Christian upbringing of Miriam. Before Miriam's mother had died, both of them had stayed with Mucina and his wife, and Miriam had heard the words of God in the little school-chapel at Mathanjiini. But a wicked heathen uncle had persecuted Miriam's mother to prevent Miriam from going to the house of God. Once he had laid a plot to kidnap Miriam. Then her brother sent her to Githumu for a time for safety and now to Kijabe to get her away from the pagan atmosphere of a Kikuyu village.

Shortly after Miriam arrived, two other small girls came from Mathanjiini, Priscilla Wanjiku, who already had been put through the circumcision rites, and Ellen Kanjiku, who was never to undergo them. Ruguru was another of the first girls to be enrolled. She was escorted to the school by her brother, an older boy who had attended the Kijabe school and to whom his destitute mother and her small family had come. They presented a note from the missionary *Bibi* who worked among the women.

> Will you admit this small girl to the girls' school? Her mother, a widow, has struggled on trying to support her small children. The burden has overcome her. She died of pneumonia today.

Ruguru stood in the dooryard in a dress of goatskins awaiting the verdict. She was assigned to a place to sleep in the small girls' dormitory. So the Kikuyu girls came—from the outdistricts, from the upcountry squatters on farms where there were no schools, from all parts of Kikuyuland—of all ages, and for a variety of reasons.

Elementary domestic science classes were organized to lay foundations for training Christian wives and mothers in the development and care of Christian homes. Foundation training for future teachers, nurses, and midwives was given. The girls marched across the ravine every morning to the station school for instruction in the three R's, but all other classes were held on their own grounds. They all "majored" in agriculture, being given teaching in better agricultural methods, which resulted in the harvesting of bumper crops from their school gardens, supplying a large percentage of the food consumed by the school.

To teach the girls the value of the equipment they used, they were paid for the work they did, whether it was in their own gardens or in the kitchen of the *Bibis.* Out of what they received for this, they paid for their slates and blankets, their soap, oil, and uniforms, or whatever other supplies were issued to them. The school flourished under this system and soon was filled to the bursting point with 170 on the roll.

While I was on furlough, Johana and Keige had moved their family to Kijabe, where he had been admitted to the Bible school for a period of Bible instruction and simple theological teaching combined with practical Christian work in and around the mission. We found him an invaluable help to us in dealing with and calming the angry parents who came to seize their daughters from the school. There was Ndundu whose village was near the village of Johana's father and who in all probability saw the first gleam of hope through the ministry of Johana and Keige at Komothai. When she saw the sheep and goats of old Njuguna—who lived in a neighboring village, who was older than her father, and who had a number of wives—being brought from time to time to her village, she became suspicious and secretly began to make inquiries of her friends among the warrior class.

"Yes, you will be bought by Njuguna," they said. But they encouraged her to refuse him.

Ndundu wept many secret tears as her hopes of becoming the wife of a young Mugikuyu were dashed to the ground. Then in her misery she thought of Keige and Johana. One moonlight night when the members of her village were fast asleep and all Kikuyuland was quiet, she took a string bag of cooked food from where she had hidden it and crept through the bushes in the direction of Kijabe. In the early morning she was received warmly at the home of Johana and Keige, who still had vivid memories of her own similar experience. She and Johana listened to her story with sympathetic interest.

"Keige will cook some gruel for you," said Johana with his encouraging smile, "and then I will take you over to the girls' school and we will talk to the *Bibi.*"

Ndundu was admitted, but contention and wrath filled her father's village. The affair of Ndundu's escape involved complications even beyond the flouting of parental authority. The old father had eaten some of the sheep and goats paid on Ndundu. Others had been paid to the owner of a girl he wanted to buy for Ndundu's brother. All of them would have to be paid back to old Njunguna if Ndundu refused to marry him. Ndundu's mother was beaten severely for having given birth to a rebellious girl. Remembering the girl's interest in Johana's school and the affairs of the *athungu* [white people], the father bade the mother make ready for a trip to Kijabe.

"Bring Ndundu out that I may see her," he demanded, glaring at me when I met him in the dooryard of our school.

"I will call her if you promise me you will not seize her and carry her away by force."

"She is mine," he retorted. "I paid ninety sheep for her mother. How will I get those sheep back if she refuses to go to the man who has paid for her? Besides, I have eaten some of his sheep. How can I return these? Bring her forth that I may see a girl who refuses her father's command."

"I know she is your daughter, but she is not a sheep or a cow to be sold against her will," I told him firmly. "The Lord made a difference between a girl and a cow, when He created them. He gave all men and women the power of choice. I will call Ndundu if you promise to reason with her quietly. This is not a jail. If she wishes to go home with you, we will not prevent her. But if she chooses to stay here and go to school, you may not seize her as a cat seizes a rat and carry her away."

Ndundu's father clutched his staff and beckoned to his wife to follow him.

"Come," he said, "we will go to the village of Johana and the house of the *munene wa miceni* [the head of the mission]."

Johana and Keige greeted the irate couple warmly, fed them, and when night came, found a place for them to sleep in a nearby Kikuyu village. Johana spent hours of the afternoon and evening talking to the father of Ndundu about how the many affairs that had come to Kikuyuland with the coming of the white man were changing their old ways. He put himself in the position and difficulties of the old man, pouring oil on the troubled waters, and told him what he judged was best to do. He pointed out to him that if Ndundu was forced to go back to his village, she still would refuse to become the wife of Njunguna. In all probability she would run away to Nairobi like the many girls who were running away from force in their villages now to join the harlots who lived with Indians in Nairobi or roamed the streets there.

"Your sheep and goats will be lost for sure," reasoned Johana. "Better allow her to remain here and read. She will then be bought by a boy who is walking in the same path she walks. He will come to your village and make a bargain with you. Was that not the way with Keige and me? Did she not run away from her father's village to go to the *miceni?* But did I not pay the dowry to her father?"

"Ha, ha, ha," laughed Keige loudly. "*Tiitheru* [of a truth], he did that."

The father of Ndundu listened intently, pulled his blanket around him more firmly, took a pinch of snuff from the goat's horn on a chain hanging from his neck, and after a long snuff which brought water to his eyes, he said:

"*Tiitheru* [of a truth], are your customs here at the *miceni* thus? Then we return to our village. We leave Ndundu here in your care. See to it that she is not bought by a worthless man who will refuse to pay sheep and goats for all the trouble she has caused us."

"You talked to him with great *kihoto* [argument not to be refuted]," said Keige proudly as she brewed a cup of tea to refresh Johana after their visitors had left.

Johana stepped into the breach in emergencies such as the case of Ndundu. The versatile Kihoga was our headman, attending to various and sundry affairs about the school that required the hand of a man. But the problems involved in the daily discipline of 170 girls of all ages and all varieties of dispositions were altogether too heavy and complicated to be carried by the two *Bibis.*

"Let us try a simple form of student government," one of us said one day as we discussed the current crop of rule-breaking and disobedience before us to be dealt with.

That evening we explained a plan to a group of the more advanced, mature Christian girls and asked them to choose from their number to act as a student council. They would hear all cases requiring discipline, decide the corrective treatment to be given, and serve for one school term of three months. One or both *Bibis* would serve with them on the council. Johana and the church elders were to be called to assist in judgment passed upon serious offenses.

"Some girl has been taking roasting ears from the school garden," reported a member of the council at one of their sessions. "We suspect a new girl who has just been admitted."

"Appoint Njeri who sleeps in her dormitory room to keep an eye on her evenings after school," suggested another.

Two days later a string bag of roasting ears was produced at mealtime when all girls were present.

"Who stole these ears from the girls' garden?" asked a member of the council.

"I took it from the new girl who came from upcountry last week," replied Njeri.

"Stand up," shouted the girls to the thief. "*He,* do you not know we planted that corn? Did you cultivate it all these months? *He,* what right have you, a very new girl, to break off roasting ears?"

The offender bowed her head in shame.

"What shall be done to her?" asked a council girl.

"We will all beat her," they cried.

"She is a new girl and has never lived with Christians before," said another. "We should forgive her this first time and tell her it will go ill with her if she returns to take food from our gardens."

"*Nigwo, nigwo* [that is it, that is it]," shouted all the girls.

"And we will take these ears to the cooks and tell them to shell and cook the corn with our supper corn," the council girls decided.

Thus were many affairs dealt with by the student council to the satisfaction of all and the correction of many. Miriam, Priscilla, Ellen, and Ruguru, with many others, advanced rapidly in stature, mind, and spirit. They were the pride of their teachers' hearts. Many Christian young men were sending the girls they had chosen to be their wives to the school to be trained before marriage so that their homes might be established with a higher standard of living and their children reared more intelligently in the knowledge of God.

It soon became apparent that we could not give the girls a practical training in home management when they were living crowded into large dormitory rooms. It was necessary to have a model practice house, and its construction and furnishings must be simple enough to be within the means of the ordinary Kikuyu man. Under the supervision of a Kikuyu Christian who was a clever carpenter, the girls set about building such a house.

As there are few level spots on Kijabe station, a tremendous amount of digging was required in order to get a level foundation, but the girls worked with willing hearts. They dug a foundation six feet deep at the back and moved the earth forward by hand until it was level. They cut bamboo poles on the top of Kijabe hill and carried them two miles downhill to split and nail them inside and outside on the framework of cedar trees. The space between the bamboo halves they filled with mud which became almost as hard as cement when it dried, making the walls strong and windproof. Rafters from the Kijabe sawmill and corrugated iron for the roof were among the few items which a Kikuyu man would have to buy with shillings.

The inside was divided into four rooms, two for sleeping, one for living, and one for cooking. A common fireplace opened into both of the latter and became the place for cooking in the kitchen. Most of the furniture was made of boxes and other odds and ends which the girls were taught to utilize. Barrel chairs were covered neatly with bright cloth. Coverings for the rough Swahili beds were made from scraps of material from the sewing classes. After classroom lessons on homemaking, the girls took turns, four at a time, living in this house for a month to prove whether or not they had learned to keep a Christian home in good order.

"*Tütheru* [of a truth], the fame of this our school is very great," said the girls to each other after one of their schoolmates had been claimed by her suitor and sent off to give light and warmth to a Christian home after her wedding in the church.

Chapter 24

THE GATHERING OF THE STORM

"THE KINYONA BOYS ARE HERE," announced Njeri the cook one day after she had located me in the girls' sewing room removing a broken needle from their machine. "They say they want to talk to you about troubles that are taking hold of the Kikuyu people."

"Where are the boys?"

"They are at the home of Waitara. They have sent his boy over to ask when you can see them."

"Tell him I will see them this evening after supper."

Njeri had washed the dishes and finished her evening work in the kitchen. The girls had met for their evening prayers and were seated in groups around the small fires built along the path, sheltered by a lean-to bamboo roof extending from the hillside. When the last bell rang, they scampered away to roll up their blankets. Then, taking a lantern, I went out to snap a large padlock in the hasp of each dormitory door to protect them from marauders. When I returned, the Kinyona boys were standing in the path of the entrance to my kitchen.

"Come in, come in," I invited them, giving each boy a hearty Kikuyu handshake. "Njeri has left a good fire in the kitchen stove. I know how you boys like to sit around a fire in the evening."

The boys filed into the kitchen, which was warm and cozy in contrast to the chilly night air outdoors in the high altitude.

"Come, bring the Kikuyu stools from the living room," I told them as I looked around for seats, "and here is a bench for two of you. Now we will have a quiet talk, and you will tell me all the affairs of Kinyona."

Thus we settled ourselves by the fireside, while the light of the lantern on the table lit up a circle of faces, solemn with serious thought. A decade ago I had seen these boys, then in the first strength of their young manhood, turn courageously away from the Kikuyu way of life to walk in the path of a Christian. They had been persecuted bitterly by their families, hated, and cursed. They had been among those who were gathered together in that Bible class at Kinyona where I had sought to teach them the Christian manner of life and prepare them for baptism.

Every member of the group had declared himself to be against all Kikuyu customs that were detrimental to the Christian walk, and they had continued to follow the way of light. But great changes were taking place all over Kikuyuland, and conflicting voices were clamoring for their attention as they sought to mold their lives in this new way and to teach their people to do likewise. There were no missionaries at Kinyona now. It was natural that these six of the strongest Christian leaders there should be sent to Kijabe to seek advice from the elders of the parent church in the matters that were troubling them, and also that they should be here by the fireside unburdening their problems to an old friend, for the tie that bound our hearts together in Christian fellowship was a strong one.

"There is trouble in Kikuyuland," they began. "We see that many of the Agikuyu who say they are Christians are Christians only in name. They want only the wisdom of the white man. They think it will help them to become rich. They are asking for education for this same reason. They say they will never rest until their land is returned or the white man driven out. They want higher wages. The leaders of the K. C. A. want all the Agikuyu to take a strong hand against the mission churches in the affair of the circumcision of girls. They say the churches have no right to forbid this custom. They are even making dangerous threats of what they will do to the white people and the black people who oppose them. *Bibi,* is it wrong for us to want our children to be educated in order to progress and be able to take good positions like the white people? We want them to be able to live in better homes than we have, and we want to provide better clothing for them than we are able to buy. Is it bad for Christians to have these desires? *Bibi,* we are confused. We do not know what to think or do."

The confusion of the Kinyona Christians was not surprising, for the whole Kikuyu tribe was in a state of transition. Revolutionary forces from the outside world were making an impact that was felt across the whole continent of Africa. It was impossible that these diligent, high-spirited people of the Kenya ridges, with their intricately interwoven systems of spirit-worship and tribal government, should retain their primitive self-sufficiency.

The most revolutionary force of all was the Gospel of Jesus Christ which had been brought to the Agikuyu, reaching remote villages long before Western civilization had begun to leave its imprint upon them. It was a light that penetrated the darkness of the ages in which the god of this world had held the Agikuyu captive at his will. His dominion over them was undisputed until the words of God fell on their ears, and a few dared to declare themselves free from his rule. Then boys like Johana, Mucai, and Paul Njunguna, having been liberated from pagan bondage, had gone out into the dark places of Kikuyuland with their Gospel torchlights until so many were being attracted by the light that their demands hardly could be met.

It was unthinkable that the one-time sovereign of these ridges would permit such an invasion of his realm to go unchallenged— and how subtle were the powers of darkness as they schemed and chose ways and means to black out the light and break down by means of discouragement, discontent, and persecution the torchlights that had blazed the way through the strongholds of Kikuyu darkness and bondage! When these first strategies failed to extinguish the light, the god of this world began to lay a master plan that called for all of his resources of diabolical subtlety, and now the conflict between the forces of light and darkness was rapidly approaching one of the series of crises that would lead eventually to such dark deeds and devastation on the ridges as neither the old Kikuyu elders nor their European rulers could have envisioned in their wildest flights of imagination.

The Kikuyu church was growing rapidly. Centers of light were springing up everywhere. The landowners who had given the land on which to build the chapel-schools often were among the first to believe and then to become leaders of the little bands of Christians. As in Kikuyu tribal life they had looked up to their tribal elders, so now they looked up to these who had become spiritual elders and preachers in their Sunday services.

As yet there was no formal church organization within the sphere of our own mission and no ordained pastors, although some of the established Christians whose testimony was vigorous and whose gifts were appropriate carried on many of the functions of a pastor, as did Johana now at Kijabe. The mission stations of Githumu and Kijabe had become the district centers for the many flourishing outschools and chapels that surrounded them. Matara and Kinyona were being carried on as outstations with Kikuyu Christians in charge. The elders of all the outdistricts came monthly to Githumu or Kijabe for a day of prayer and to bring in their offerings, which were distributed for the support of the teacher-evangelists, and to engage in palavers over affairs connected with their church life. The New Testament in Kikuyu was in circulation, and the entire Bible was available in Swahili, the trade language used throughout East Africa. Scores of Christian homes had been established. Many of the early Christians now had families growing up unshackled by the chains of darkness that had bound their parents.

Under cover of this rapid church growth, the enemy was carrying out a part of his master plan, for he was busy developing many counterfeit Christians to be used as a spearhead in his all-out attack on the forces of light. Hundreds of schoolboys and girls arose in the Sunday services to confess Christ as Saviour and to say they wanted to walk in the path of God. They were instructed carefully in catechumen classes before baptism, but who could tell the true from the false? By this time the pleasant by-products of the Gospel had gained so much popularity with keen-minded, progressive young Kikuyu that they willingly gave a superficial adherence to Christianity in order to partake of its practical benefits.

There was no attempt on the part of the missionaries to destroy that in Kikuyu tribal life which was not unbecoming to a follower of Christ, but it was necessary to point out to the believers their need to forsake the immorality, drunkenness, and witchcraft in which they had been reared. The dowry system of marriage was not called into question, or interfered with, yet the physical disabilities that followed the circumcision of Kikuyu girls became so apparent that a stand had to be taken against this custom.

As early as 1916 a neighboring missionary society in Kikuyuland, backed by its African leaders, had forbidden the practice of this custom within the church. Ten years later even the Government made an attempt to secure a modificaton of the operation, but it was not until 1930 that legislation was passed which enabled the courts to take effective action against the performance of this mutilation against the will of a girl or her parents. In the meantime the church was strengthening her stand on this issue in every missionary society. Men of maturing Christian discernment, such as Johana, were one with the missionaries in their opposition to this heathen custom. Those who had professed the name of Christ were not being admitted now to full church membership without promising to outlaw the practice within the circle of their family jurisdiction and to abstain from polygamy and other Kikuyu customs inconsistent with a true Christian walk.

It was here that the enemy's ranks of counterfeit Christians rose up in defiance. They had welcomed the surface changes brought about by the Gospel, they had been attracted by its comforts, but they could not tolerate the searchlight it directed on the darkness that bound their still pagan hearts. Its straight and narrow path was not for them. The church, said they, had no right to prohibit age-old customs which were essential to the welfare of the tribe. The old enemy of pioneer days had known where to train his forces and had prepared the roundup that would call them to their true colors. So it came about that the leaders and many of their followers in the subversive movements already abroad upon the ridges were one-time mission adherents and recipients of the highest education of their time—among them some of the most brilliant young minds of Kikuyuland.

At this period church and school still were largely synonymous terms, for the many little bush schools had as their main motive teaching the people to read the Word of God, so that the elements of reading and writing, plus much instruction about the affair of God and the path to His heavenly village, occupied almost their entire attention. They were evangelizing centers rather than schools in the true sense of the word. A few advanced mission schools existed in Kikuyuland. It was to one of these, a complete grammar school conducted by the Scotch Presbyterian Mission, that Muthungu and his brother Waitara, with Githae and Mucai's young sister, Nyambura, had been sent in 1922, for the schools at our two main stations in Kikuyuland, while they had progressed farther than the bush schools, offered training that would not be comparable to more than that of the third grade.

Government did not yet have an educational program of its own. Its interest in mission schools was confined to the few advanced ones which it subsidized to some degree. However, about 1925, the Jeanes School at Kabete was instituted to train teachers to do a work similar to that done by the Jeanes teachers in the United States, who organized and conducted schools of Negroes in the backward rural sections of the South. Muthungu was a member of one of the first classes to enter the new center at Kabete, and he developed into an extremely capable teacher.

In this new era of enlightenment in which the old system of Kikuyu communal life was slowly breaking down, the god of this world found additional means which might be employed to hold the Agikuyu in his grip. The arrival of the white man to make his home in their midst had brought great changes to the Kikuyu way of life, which never would be the same again. Many young Agikuyu, as Gacingiri and Mwenja who were sitting here with us tonight, had worked in Nairobi or on European farms. They had tasted of the exciting new way of life the white people had brought to their borders, a life far removed from round thatched huts, warrior dances, and Kikuyu palavers, and new ambitions stirred within them.

The boys who came back from the first world war, having had a glimpse beyond the Kikuyu horizon, were fired with desires to cultivate their ancestral lands, increase their possessions, and live like other people in the world. Better houses were replacing the old ones. New manual skills were being acquired. Some were working at clerical jobs, as Githae at the Government post at Fort Hall. Improved methods of farming and new crops were being adopted by some. Others, like Thiga, our herdman of Kinyona days, were acquiring better breeds of cattle and enriching themselves thereby. The young people were flocking to the townships and the towns in search of material betterment. A new paganism was being designed by the powers of darkness to deceive and enslave the mass of Kikuyu men and boys who had followed the first rays of light that led them out of their pagan bondage to the bush schools with their liberating teaching of the Word of God. The new paganism was a lust for wealth, pleasure, and progress, with an indifference to the things of the Spirit.

Another change was taking place on the ridges which helped to forward the enemy's designs. The tribal lands of the Agikuyu were becoming too congested for a people whose economy still revolved around their livestock and who required large grazing lands as well as land to farm. The medical help received from both Government and mission sources had been no small factor in bringing about the increase of population, for yaws and smallpox, great killers in the past, now were virtually stamped out. The famines that once periodically wiped out great masses of the Kikuyu people no longer followed years of drought, for quantities of food were brought by the Government to the stricken areas to sustain the people until new crops could be raised.

The rate of infant mortality was dropping rapidly, due to the care that was given to many women at the time of childbirth and the medical help that was available for their babies. In addition to what was being done along this line by missions, the Government had established a large maternity training center at Pumwani. Hanna Nyambura, who was now at the home of her brother, Mucai, helping the Kinyona women and girls to make their clothes and teaching them to walk in the Christian way, was soon to enter this Pumwani center to train as a midwife.

Europeans were settling in greater numbers in the fertile highlands. The squatters on the lands they occupied were multiplying both as to families and livestock until they found their quarters cramped, yet there was no room for them in the already congested native reserves. In all this atmosphere of progress, change, and growth, there were many elements of discontent on which the powers of darkness were only too glad to capitalize as they mustered their forces against the forces of light. It was grievances concerning the land, some just and some exaggerated, that had been fanned into flame in the Harry Thuku riot of 1922. Harry Thuku was still in exile, but the Kikuyu Central Association of which he had been the secretary was flourishing again after having gone underground for a short time following the deportation of its leader.

Now the secretary of the K. C. A. was one, Jomo Kenyatta, who was also editor of the organization's periodical newspaper and whose name was to come into world-wide prominence a little more than two decades later. Closely associated with him in its leadership were Jesse Kariuki and Joseph Kangethe. They were young intellectuals of the new Kikuyu age, all of them at one time, adherents of some mission where they had received their early schooling but wholly unchanged in their pagan sympathies at heart. Up and down the ridges, into the villages and townships, among the squatters on the European farms traveled representatives of the K. C. A., speaking, organizing, and in the name of progress and the welfare of the great Kikuyu tribe, subtly spreading a propaganda that eventually would stir the people to rise up to shake off the shackles of the white man in defense of their ancient beliefs and their tribal lands.

These political agitators were ready material to work into

the plans of the powers of darkness in their opposition to the forceful stand that true Christians had taken against the time-honored customs of polygamy and the circumcision of girls. So strong was the feeling on these issues that whole outschools pulled away from their parent missions to run their own affairs and to establish their own churches in which they used the Christian Scriptures and hymns (with modifications to suit their own interests) and in which polygamy and the circumcision of girls were strong tenets.

The independent schools and churches, some of which began as early as the time of the Harry Thuku riot in 1922, were headed largely by malcontents among professing Christians, many of them under church discipline. They had drawn with them a large body of the semicivilized counterfeit Christians who were filling the mission churches. They propagated themselves by the same methods that were used by bearers of the true Gospel light. Independent bush schools were growing in numbers and strength, smiled upon and encouraged by the K. C. A., which by now was so dominating them that the two movements, linked together in the minds of the people but not officially connected, had become close accomplices in forwarding the master strategy of the prince of darkness. One of the strongest independent centers was on the hillside just above Kijabe mission station.

The Kikuyu independent churches had formed themselves into several organizations under different names, one of which was assisted in its organization by an archbishop of a South African Separatist Church who had been called to Kenya for the purpose. A number of preachers had been prepared for ordination and were licensed by him to preach and baptize. Very recently a great independent baptismal service had been held at the Chania River. Candidates who were husbands of more than one wife, the bishop said, were eligible for baptism. After elders buried the candidates in the waters of the Chania and brought them to a stand on their feet, the bishop made a cross with white chalk on their foreheads, gave them a new name, and called upon God with a loud voice to bless the baptized one. The candidates were relieved at not having to make promises as to Christian conduct or to testify about what had taken place in their hearts since they had decided to embrace Christianity, as the people of the *miceni* did. Before they were allowed to put on dry clothes, someone among their relatives or friends had to be prepared to give the bishop's henchman a ten-shilling note to pay for the baptism.

The Kikuyu boys who sat by the kitchen fire talked long and earnestly with me about all these affairs that were abroad in Kikuyuland, both the good and the bad. They had heard the speeches of the K. C. A., subtle in their apparent spirit of patriotism and progress, and they were conscious of the undercurrent of unrest. It was this that caused them to say:

"*Bibi,* we are confused. We know not what to think or do."

"It is not wrong for Christians to want to progress," was the sum of the advice that I gave them in the course of our long conversation. "When God by His Spirit transplants a person from the kingdom of darkness into the kingdom of light, that person desires to live on a higher plane both physically and spiritually. The mistake is to value the desires for better things above our desire for spiritual development and progress. *Jesu* said, 'Seek ye *first* the kingdom of God, and his righteousness; and *all these things* shall be added unto you.'

"Many of us know about the Agikuyu loss of land. Through the Alliance of Protestant Missions, the missionaries work on your behalf along many lines. You must remember the K. C. A. is made up of Agikuyu who are not willing to admit and turn from their sins and mistakes. They are opposed to the teachings of the New Testament and are seeking to pervert the Christian way of life by undermining all church activity.

"Tell the Kinyona people the Lord works for those who

wait upon Him. To trust in political agitators who are out of touch with God will lead the Agikuyu back into great darkness. Walk in the light while you have the light. Let us all stand together in prayer to God. He will keep us true and show us His way when we are perplexed."

"*Tiitheru* [of a truth], these words are words of wisdom. We have laid them to heart," responded the Kinyona boys.

"Now let us go that you may sleep in order that we may return to come another day," said Mwenja as the boys rose to leave.

"Greet all the Kinyona people. Tell them to remember the words of the hymn they sing in Kikuyu:

> "Hold the fort, for I am coming,"
> *Jesu niatwirire* [Jesus has told us];
> Wave the answer back to Heaven,
> "By Thy grace we will."

"We will tell them," they said. "*Tigwo na uhoro* [abide with peace]."

Chapter 25

THE STORM BREAKS IN FURY

AFTER NEARLY THREE YEARS of progress in the training of Kikuyu girls, shadows began to cloud the bright future of the Kijabe school. Some members of the girls' council at that time were not as keen as others had been. Matters of discipline in the school grew more difficult. The overflowing spirit of joy, happy fellowship, and co-operation was disappearing, yet the *Bibis* could not put their fingers on any one thing that was responsible for the change in the atmosphere of the school. The growing spirit of restlessness and disobedience reached a climax near the end of the last term of 1928.

One day when the *Bibi* on dining-room duty went out to see that the girls were all in order for the noonday meal, not a girl was in sight except the cooks. The food that was dished out on the long tables had been left untouched.

"*Airetu ni mekurega kuria irio* [the girls refuse to eat their food]," explained the cooks.

"Where are the girls?" asked the *Bibi.*

"*Me rui* [they are down by the river]."

The girls had gone off to hold a secret meeting. Little by little the truth trickled out about what had been going on in the ranks during the past months as the girls were being affected by what was going on around them on the ridges. The tide of feeling against the church rules regarding the circumcision of girls was running high, and wild talk was flying about Kikuyuland.

One story was abroad to the effect that the Son of God had been sacrificed many years ago and some day would return. A Kikuyu mother would give birth to Him again. He would deliver the Agikuyu from the wicked hand of the Europeans and would become King of the Agikuyu, who would reign with Him over all of Europe. The story told how the Europeans knew about this coming event and, seeking means to save themselves, had forbidden the circumcision of Kikuyu girls. This would result in *thahu* [uncleanness] for the girls. Their children would die in childhood, or if they lived, would be sterile. Therefore, the story said, all Agikuyu everywhere must command or even force all parents to circumcise their girls according to the custom of their forebears.

Members of the political association of young Kikuyu men were telling all Kikuyu fathers of girls to refuse to take a church vow not to circumcise their daughters. They also urged them to take their daughters from mission schools. Large sums of money were being collected to build and establish Kikuyu independent schools. On the other hand, all fathers attached to missions were being pressed to take a solemn oath, secretly, to circumcise their daughters according to all tribal customs.

The circumcision season would be at hand in the early part of the new year. It was the time of singing and dancing. Young Kikuyu men were going everywhere throughout Kikuyuland teaching the young Agikuyu a new dance to a song with words that were obscene and revolting. A large, elaborate circumcision ceremony for girls, unlike the usual Kikuyu ceremonies was being planned.

Boys who were relatives of or who were planning to marry

some of the schoolgirls and council members of Kijabe Girls' School were members of the roaming bands of Kikuyuland. Our girls were forbidden to meet boys to have talks with them secretly, but the cozy girls' sewing room was available at any time after school hours for friends to meet them and have a chat. For months, as they visited with and talked to their friends and relatives in the sewing room, the girls had been kept informed of all that was being published abroad in Kikuyuland and were being instructed thoroughly concerning the part they were expected to play in the plan to overthrow the destroyers of Kikuyu custom.

In this secret meeting by the river, the appointed girl leaders were developing their final plans to force the entire school into marching off Kijabe station with all the schoolboys in a triumphant procession at the close of the term—just two weeks hence—leaving the missionaries to make up their minds to allow light and darkness to mingle without conflict or else to let the light be extinguished by the threatened oncoming billows of darkness.

The *Bibis* were not aware of these carefully laid plans on the day of the meeting at the river. We did know, however, that to allow a spirit of disobedience to prevail would bring chaos and confusion to the school. Therefore, we decided to take drastic measures to curb it.

During the usual evening line-up that night, all but the little girls were told to march in line to the outside door of the largest dormitory room. One *Bibi* took the register and sat by a table inside. One at a time the girls were admitted by the other *Bibi.* Each girl was required to decide whether she would obey all the rules of the school and go to classes the next morning or pack her box and leave the mission grounds by daybreak. Her decision was recorded and she passed through another door into a line that had no communication with the line from which she had come. Without any hesitation, many chose to leave. None would bind themselves by a promise of obedience, for those who had a desire to do so were afraid of the others and would not commit themselves.

The hours of the night were spent by the leaders in threatening reluctant ones, explaining what would befall any girl or child if she refused to go with them when they left en masse in the morning. By schooltime the dormitories and compound were quiet and practically deserted. Wahu, one of the council members, remained and was sent to help the builders who were busy making a new stone building for the daughters of Christian parents.

As we had progressed in the training of Kikuyu girls, we had seen that it was going to be difficult to cope with the two classes of girls which we had in one school. Those who had been admitted when they were young, as Miriam, Priscilla, and Ellen, soon would be ready for advanced training and better equipment than it was wise to offer the raw girls from pagan villages who began their school life in their middle or late teens. It was probable also that, by too intimate association, these raw girls, so newly come from the degrading moral atmosphere of heathen Kikuyuland, might have an unwholesome influence on the younger girls and the daughters of Christian parents who had not been reared in paganism. Looking into the future with this realization, the new building was being prepared for the day when some consecrated woman teacher from the homeland would be sent to us to supervise a more advanced section of our school.

"Why do you continue to build?" laughed a passing Kikuyu woman in derision as she saw Wahu helping the builders. "Do you not know the schools of the *miceni* are finished?"

Standing nearby, I overheard the woman's contemptuous remark.

"We continue to build," I called, "in order to have a place

to house all the girls who will return to be trained here when the present storm of *Cetani* has passed."

By noon a number of girls came back to the dormitories. They had left with the rest because of intimidation but had gone to the villages of nearby relatives and waited until it was safe to return. Little Ruguru, who had told the *Bibi* quietly that she wanted to stay with her, had been kidnaped by some girls in the ravine when she was on her way to the station school and carried away by the crowd of girls who had left for Githumu and Mathanjiini districts, the home of her heathen relatives. It was several terms before Ruguru was able to get free and return.

Priscilla, Ellen, and Miriam had been frightened into going with the same crowd of girls. A week later, Miriam had been spanked by her brother Mucina and sent back with a letter to the *Bibi,* begging her to forgive the frightened girl and give her another chance to obey the school rules. The Christian relatives sent to escort her back said Mucina was very angry with the foolish bands of young men traveling about Kikuyuland. It was not until a Sunday afternoon during the vacation month, however, that I heard a gentle rap on the door and opened it to find Priscilla and Ellen standing before me, their faces flushed with victory. The two small girls had been taken to their heathen villages—Ellen to be circumcised—but they had escaped and traveled alone most of the way through the long, lonely, and dangerous forest trail between Mathanjiini and Kijabe.

With a small enrollment we managed to carry on as usual to the close of the term just before Christmas. Then *Bibi* Rezac took some of the girls on a safari to Githumu while I stayed on duty at Kijabe with those who could not go home for their vacation month. It was then that the storm of *Cetani* broke in all its fury upon us.

Matathia, on the hill back of Kijabe, was a strong independent school and church. It was also a center for political agitators and subversive activities. We learned afterward that secretly for months they had been perfecting plots to deal a blow at Kijabe mission that would send it reeling off its foundations and forever blot out its testimony. The church membership was being tested. Kijabe church attendance and that of the outschools dwindled as the agitators delivered to them the ultimatum of, "Join with us or take the consequences." But Johana and the old reliables were moved by none of these things. They stood firmly at their post of duty and carried on the usual services.

"The houses of the loyal Kikuyu Christians at Mukeu out-school have been stoned and their gardens destroyed," reported one of the evangelists who had been trying to speak words of peace to the people on the hill only to have them reply with stones. "The independents are trying to force them to leave the mission by persecutions of every kind. They say they will do likewise to all Africans who partake of the Lord's Supper at Kijabe church next Sunday. All the people are filled with fear."

When Sunday came, the congregation in Kijabe church was small, for fear held the people in its grip like a vice. *Bibi* Hulda Stumpf, who was the mission secretary, was asked to come to the morning service with a notebook and pencil to record the names of those who were not afraid to show their colors by taking Communion. The list of names which she wrote was not a long one.

Each succeeding day the atmosphere around Kijabe station grew more tense. Wednesday was New Year's day of 1930. In the evening I left Wangari the housegirl in charge at home, took my lantern, and crossed the ravine to the Downing home for the weekly missionary prayer meeting. *Bibi* Stumpf presided at the organ and afterward invited me over to her cottage nearby to see a new book. After we had said good night, I retraced my steps back over the athletic field, descended into the deep ravine, and climbed the hill to my rooms adjoining the girls' dormitory. Wangari was sitting on the floor beside the bedroom fireplace.

"Oh, *Bibi,*" she cried as I came in, "why are you so late, and why do you go out in the night alone? Do you not know we all live in great danger? No one knows when someone hiding behind a tree will hurl a bottle at one's head."

Wangari's people lived at Matathia. Later I knew she had good reasons to fear for my safety that night.

"I do not fear the night," I assured her as, lantern in hand, I led the way to her dormitory room, where the other girls were fast asleep.

The night passed quietly on our side of the ravine, but in the morning while I was eating breakfast, Njeri the cook came in to say that someone outside wanted to see me at once. I hurried out to find Johana there. His face was gray instead of black, and grief was written on every feature.

"*Bibi,*" he said, "*Kijabe ni kwehu* [Kijabe is bad]. I have been sent to call you to the other side. *Bibi* Stumpf was killed in the night!"

It was hard to take in the meaning of Johana's words, but I mounted my mule and rode over to the little brick cottage where I had taken leave of my friend the night before. Softly I opened the door on a shocking scene. Broken pieces of window glass and several large rocks were scattered about the room. The rocks had been taken from the retaining wall outside the bedroom window. They had broken the sash as well as the glass as they had been hurled into the room. Hulda Stumpf lay across the bed with a mattress doubled over her face. I was the second person to enter the room after the tragedy, and I made a careful examination of her poor body. She had been brutally treated but was not, as the story was circulated, the victim of a bungling attempt at circumcision. That finally she had been strangled was evident by the large black and blue patches on her throat and neck. She was safe on the other side, but had had a rough passage.

" 'Be not afraid of them that kill the body, and after that have no more that they can do,' " I murmured to myself.

The countryside was shaken as the news got around. Government officials came and went. Investigations dragged on throughout the following months with no apparent results. The old Kikuyu tribal elders were shocked and horrified that such a crime should be committed in their midst. African soldiers were sent to guard the station day and night. The girls and I were ordered to leave the school. Temporary quarters were found for us on the side of the ravine with other missionaries, where we would be less exposed to danger.

The powers of darkness, unable to endure the presence of the light in their dark domain, had wreaked their vengeance upon us, and for the moment seemed to have the upper hand. Would they be able to drive out the light and envelope Kikuyuland in complete darkness once more? We knew that the light had not shone in vain upon these ridges, for One greater than the prince of darkness had commandeed the light to shine upon them—and it would continue to shine.

Chapter 26

RECONSTRUCTION

By February it was considered safe for us to go back to the girls' school for the opening of the new term. Girls who had been forced to leave against their will drifted back to register, but half of those who had been enrolled before the walkout did not return. Most of the missing ones were from the outdistricts around Githumu. There was great interest in the school, however, among the squatters' girls living on the upcountry farms, for as yet few of the settlers were interested in the establishment of schools on their farms for their squatters' children.

The school became a busy, happy place once more, with much to learn and much to do and sure evidence of the working of the Spirit of God within the hearts of those who came to be trained. On Monday evenings I met with all the girls in the large bamboo dining room for a Gospel meeting in which the Pace Gospel cartoons were used as illustrations. Often I wished that friends in the homeland could look in upon the sea of upturned faces and sparkling eyes, wide open with keen interest as their owners caught the meaning of the message illustrated by the picture. It was cheering to see the light break in upon darkened understandings and to observe the fruits of complete change in the lives of many of the girls. Often in their testimonies during the week they spoke of the new truths learned.

By 1933, with the arrival of *Bibi* Truesdell from America, the longed-for advanced school became a reality. The old buildings were used by the refugee girls, while several units of new stone buildings had been erected for the daughters of Christian parents and the advanced Christian girls. There had been no girl teachers up to this point, so it was an eventful day when the first training class was formed with seven members. Miriam, now about seventeen, Priscilla, Ellen, and Helen the albino daughter of Chief Daudi, were among them.

For some time Muthungu's brother Waitara had been teaching the higher standards on the girls' compound. Now we took the rest of our girls from the station school, and under supervision our teacher trainees taught the lower standards for practice teaching in the mornings, getting their own lessons in the afternoons while the others were at their garden work. Helen amazed all of us by her teaching ability. The cousins, Bethi and Ruthi, also members of the first training class, were to do splendid work later on teaching in the station school at Githumu. Miriam became a tower of strength to me through the years as she lent a helping hand at administrative matters.

Already, here and there in the Christian homes of Kikuyuland, we saw our girls setting a new standard of motherhood and influencing their communities by testimony and service—and we realized afresh that our labor was not in vain.

Kibui, a bright girl from an outschool below Githumu admitted to the school at the beginning of the second year, was one of the cleverest in *Bibi* Rezac's handwork classes and a leader in all of the school's activities. She was particularly interested in preparing for hospital training. However, the boy who was paying her dowry price and whom she had agreed to marry claimed her as his bride during a school holiday. Several years later, while Kibui was in Kijabe hospital for treatment, we had a long talk togetheer. She told of the many sorrows of the women during childbirth in the district around her. She said that she was called to help them and that she did what she could, but did the *Bibi* know of a book she could buy to give her better instructions? There was such a book in Kiswahili, giving simple instructions in midwifery. This Kibui bought, studied diligently, and she was called upon far and near to help Kikuyu women over difficult times.

Helen, the albino girl, was to make good along the same line. More than ten years later I was to take a difficult maternity case to Fort Hall Government Hospital, and whom should I see there but Helen, flitting about the delivery room in a smart white uniform and flowing nursing sister's cap! A graduate of the maternity center at Pumwani, she was considered to be one of the hospital's cleverest and most efficient midwives.

Perisi Wambui was another of the early girls, now married, who had made rapid strides both mentally and spiritually during her comparatively short stay at Kijabe Girls' School. Muthungu had brought her to me one day about five years before. She was very clean but possessed clothing only sufficient to cover part of her body. She had confessed openly her faith in the Lord Jesus at a Sunday morning service at Githumu and had gone to school for a few months, but she was not far removed from the status of a pagan village girl.

"I do not know what you will think of my choice of a girl," Muthungu said hesitatingly. "My head told me to choose a girl who had some education and training to be my wife. But my heart told me to choose Wambui. What do you think of this affair?"

"I think," I replied, "that in the affair of the choice of a life companion it is safer to follow the leadings of your heart than those of your head."

Muthungu looked relieved.

"Could you admit Wambui to your training school?" he

asked. "Would you train her in the ways you train Kikuyu girls to be intelligent Christian wives and mothers? I do not wish to marry her until she has learned how to make and care for a good Christian home."

"I will be pleased to admit her at the beginning of next term."

A year or so later, after a beautiful Christian wedding and a reception held on our grounds, the girls had sent Muthungu and Wambui on their way to Kinyona with many prayers and good wishes to found another Christian home amid the pagan villages of Kinyona district, where Muthungu was to teach.

A year and a half after their wedding day, Muthungu and Wambui sat in my kitchen. Wambui was holding a beautiful six-months-old girl in her arms near the warmth of the kitchen stove. Baby Helen had sickened suddenly and become very ill in their isolated home. No medical help was available, and they had despaired of her life. The love for their first-born was strong. Their heartstrings were torn with grief and fear as they watched and prayed beside her for two days and two nights. On the third day they had set off through the forest and over the plains in search of medical aid. Now they had reached their journey's end. Little Helen still lived, and hope revived.

"I will give you a note to Dr. and Mrs. Davis at the hospital," I told them. "Wambui probably will have to go into the hospital with Helen. They will do everything possible to restore her to health."

But it was too late to save the life of little Helen. Meningitis had done its deadly work of destruction in the membranes enveloping her brain. After a week Muthungu and Wambui returned to their faraway home sorrowful, yet not as others sorrow who have no hope.

Now they were at Kijabe once more, living temporarily in the girls' bamboo practice house, for Muthungu had been called to meet an urgent need for teachers in the station school.

It was here that their son and heir, Davis, had been born to gladden their hearts. What great care and devotion were bestowed upon him! What thoughtful planning for his future good and highest development! The question of circumcision still was a burning topic of discussion among Kikuyu Christians. They wondered if the circumcision of boys during babyhood would deliver them from temptation later on when they reached the age of the tribal rites.

Muthungu and Wambui were the first parents at Kijabe to decide in favor of this break with Kikuyu custom and had the operation performed on their son at the hospital before he was a month old. Through the years Wambui was to prove over and over again the power of living faith in Christ and her value as a patient and understanding companion. In the face of difficulties, and even at times when Muthungu would be overcome with the desires of his old nature and the confusing forces about him, Wambui was to stand triumphant over every circumstance.

So we went on training girls, seeking by the power of God to prepare them physically, mentally, and spiritually to become bearers of light and messengers of the love of Christ to the women on the ridges of Kikuyuland. Term after term to the present day an endless succession of Kikuyu girls has filled the dormitories and classrooms with laughter and tears, conflict, triumph, and praise. One day Miriam was helping me to choose those to be admitted from a long line of applicants. She indicated a tall, willowy girl and asked me if I knew her.

"Have I ever seen this one?" I asked in return, touching the girl on the shoulder.

Miriam laughed.

"Is she not Nyakiega, the baby you rescued when she was left in the hut to die with her mother near Githumu?"

How wonderful are the ways of God! My mind flew back to the night of the village meeting near Githumu when one of the men, under protest, had taken me to a hut at the back of the village where a wee mite of skin and bones was tugging at the dry breast of her dying mother. The life that had been saved that night was now to be trained for Him.

"Sarah, Hanna, and Naomi, the daughters of Johana are coming for training this term," announced Miriam another time.

"I am glad to hear you say the daughters of Johana are coming to our school. They have been spared the conflicts with the powers of darkness that their parents faced. Johana and Keige overcame fear, superstition, and the curses of their parents when they stepped out of heathenism to walk in the light. We now see the powers of darkness preparing other dangers to ensnare the children of the first Christian parents."

"What dangers, *Bibi,* do you see to be surrounding our generation of young Africans?" asked Miriam.

"I see every phase of African tribal life being changed by the influence of a godless, man-made civilization empowered by the god of this world. Young boys will be tempted to go to the towns like Nairobi to look for work. Girls will leave their villages to seek an easier way of life, better food, fine clothes. This will lead them to lives of sin and shame. Young Africans leaving their tribal homes or mission schools will hear many words which will fill their hearts with discontent, strife, and bitterness, leading them to doubt the love of God and His way of salvation through faith in His Son. The founding of Christian homes and Christian schools to establish young Africans in the Word of God so they will be able to discern between the true and the false is the affair that will save Africa from being deceived by the false standards of a godless civilization from the West. Is this not the aim of our school?"

"*Tüitheru* [of a truth]," replied Miriam thoughtfully. "We girls who have been taught the way of truth hope to do our part to make homes of this kind."

Chapter 27

LIGHT OVERSHINES THE DARKNESS

THE KIJABE CHRISTIAN women had come together as usual one Thursday afternoon in the early 1930's. To lend a guiding hand to this weekly meeting was one of my responsibilities. The women were a motley crowd. Some had learned to read and write in outschools, had married, and moved in to live on Kijabe mission station. A few had had a scanty training of a few terms in Kijabe Girls' School before marriage. Others had been married from pagan villages and could neither read nor write. They had been testifying of their difficulties and burdens and had asked prayer for strength to follow *Mwathani* (the Lord). Suddenly small, wrinkled Leah, her bright eyes flashing, called out from her seat on the side-lines:

"You meet here week after week to talk about your troubles and lack of strength. Do you ever do anything to help others to find the light? Do you ever pray with the women living up on the hill? I never hear of your walking out to Mukeu to help those women grow strong in faith. Over at Metumi where I came from the Christian women met at different centers each week. They grew strong in faith and were filled with joy."

Leah had been a spiritual force in our midst ever since she

had joined the household of her son-in-law, our teacher Waitara. She was a veteran in the faith who had learned to follow the path of God at a distant village where a neighboring mission had carried the Gospel light. Silence followed her forceful remarks. The thought was a new one. It took a little time to understand what Leah meant to infer. Finally the leader of the meeting stood up.

"You have heard what Leah says. *Mukuug'atia* [what do you say]?" she asked the women.

"We are taught to help others and seek the lost," responded Sarah the wife of Mucege.

Then Keige of Johana got to her feet.

"You women know we are a lazy lot in the work of *Mwathani* [the Lord]," she said. "*Tiitheru* [of a truth], we think only of ourselves. Could we not all meet on the hill one week, call those women to meet with us at Mukeu the next week, and all meet at Kijabe the third week?"

A new chapter in the women's activity was begun that day. The group meetings at the three centers increased in numbers and were alive with enthusiasm. In seeking to strengthen the hands of other women in the Lord, each was finding her own burdens had grown lighter. In a few months they were talking of another meeting. Why could they not all meet together at Mukeu and invite Christian women to come from other centers and other missions? They would invite women to come as guest speakers and meet for three or four days. It was a new idea. Not many fellowship conferences had been held in Kenya up to this time, and none that brought together the believers of more than closely adjacent localities. For women to congregate from any distance for such a purpose and lead their own meetings was unheard-of.

"But where would we sleep?" asked one doubter.

"What would we eat?" asked another.

"*He!*" cried Leah. "Is there not a large old building standing near the chapel at Mukeu? Will you not all go to repair that building and make it fit for sleeping quarters for all?"

"As for food," added Sarah, "if we all took food and stored it with our village sisters, we should not lack for food for our guests for three days. We could each give some of our money for a *mondo* [a bag] from which to buy meat, tea, sugar, and bread."

"*Tüitheru, nigwo, nigwo* [of a truth, it is so, it is so]," chorused the leading women while the doubters lapsed into silence to await developments.

Several weeks later, when plans for the first women's conference to be held at Mukeu were well under way, Johana and two of the church elders called on me in great concern.

"We hear the women have plans for a conference at Mukeu," they began.

"Yes, that is true."

"Well, you know, *Bibi,* Kikuyu women never have been known to manage so large an affair. You do not know our women as we know them. If you do not have some men about to manage the food supply, the women will disagree and quarrel and spoil their meeting. Choose some of the elders to be in the midst to keep order and to command the women."

The women did not refuse to invite several of the elders to inspect their preparations. They had cut and piled up a supply of wood. The roof of the old building had been repaired and its floor covered with a thick layer of dry banana leaves which were to serve as the community bed. Each woman was told to bring her blanket. As Kikuyu women were not supposed to know the affair of meat, the elders were asked to buy their supply of meat and tea and sugar for them. However, as to the affair of having the elders in their midst to keep order and direct them, they demonstrated to the great amazement and guarded acknowledgment of their menfolk that they could handle the other matters with joyous harmony and remarkable efficiency.

The opening day arrived. *Bibi* Moody, *Bibi* Holman, and I climbed the hill to Mukeu on our mules while a small delegation of girls from the school followed us in single file, each with her blanket and extra dresses in a bundle on her head. The invited guests began to arrive about noon amid the shouts of hilarious welcome. The hymn singing at the opening meeting at 2:30 was indeed a joyful noise unto the Lord. Introductions and words of welcome were the order, and then a short message from the Word by Sarah. The meeting closed in a spirit of great anticipation of a blessing from *Mwathani* (the Lord).

The outstanding message of the next day was brought by Miriam, the wife of Ben. She had been one of the promising refugee girls at Kijabe when I went to take charge of that work for a brief period in 1919. Miriam had tramped with other women through many miles of forest and bamboos, over rivers, valleys, and ridges, to reach Mukeu. She spoke as one inspired with a message from the Word to the hearts of the women.

During a testimony hour, a woman from an outschool district stood up with a beaming face and declared:

"I belong to *Jesu.* He has bought me with His blood. My Kikuyu owners have sold my body for sheep and goats, but they can never sell my heart. I am His forever."

Messages given by the women from other missions were most helpful. A sense of oneness in Christ Jesus and a unity in the task of bringing to Kikuyu womanhood the good news of salvation from sin and death prevailed throughout. The last evening meeting, before the morning when they would separate to go their several ways to their villages, closed with hymns of praise and glowing testimonies. The women were singing as they left the church. Outside they were like women filled with new wine. Spontaneously joining hands, they formed a circle and marched around, singing and praising God as they marched, loath to leave the mount of blessing.

"The awakening of the Kikuyu women is a real miracle," remarked *Bibi* Moody as our safari journeyed back to Kijabe from the conference. "A few years ago, who would have thought it possible?"

"Did you ever hear a message such as Miriam *wa* Ben of Githumu gave?" I returned. "The conference will be a sure incentive to our schoolgirls to carry on the good work in the years to come."

The decade that followed the black storms of *Cetani* in 1929 was marked by sunshine on a growing church. Chastened by persecution, it was a purified body that continued to develop in the knowledge of God, in the shouldering of responsibility, and enlargement of vision—while the independent movement continued to absorb, under its compromising system, many who were satisfied with the mere by-products of Christianity. When the Kenya summer season at the end of 1936 and the beginning of 1937 was approaching, the Kijabe church elders were meeting in one of their regular sessions.

"It has been a long time since we had an African conference at Kijabe," said one elder to the others.

"And should we not gather together to praise and thank God now that we have been delivered from the people of lies in our midst, that our numbers are increasing, and our church is growing stronger than ever?" another responded.

"*Tiitheru* [of a truth]," agreed Johana, "it is becoming that we should call for a conference for the coming season. We will call for some of our *athungu* [white people] friends to meet with us, and we will call our African friends from other parts—from Ukambaland and Masailand and those from other missions. Let us ask permission and blessing of God in order that we may be blessed indeed. Then we may think of committees and plans."

The missionary who had the oversight of the Kijabe station and church, pleased with the elders' plans, met with them to advise and co-operate. Leading African women were invited to sit with the elders on their committees. I was asked to send out invitations far and wide to the districts, tribes, and other missions they had indicated. The elders wanted their own hearts revived, and they prayed that all who came to Kijabe would be so revived that, when they returned home to report, the people of their districts would be rekindled with fire from above.

"Many people will come," they said. "The church is too small. Where will the people sit?"

"We will bring bamboo poles from the forest on the hill," said one of the elders. "In that level place under the wild olive trees east of the chapel we will build an out-of-doors meeting place, with a platform for the speakers. We will make a kitchen on the side and put a stove in it to cook the food the Kijabe Christians will bring in for the guests."

Prayer continued, expectations of a time of blessing increased as the preparations were carried out, and great crowds assembled in the comfortable, picturesque amphitheater for the opening service, with Johana as the chairman. A message by Munyaka from Kangundo in Ukambaland, the oldest outstation of the Africa Inland Mission, went home to hearts with great force as he told of Rebekah's loving her bridegroom through the testimony of the servant and consenting to the long desert journey to go with him and climaxed it with a vivid description of her meeting with Isaac and its application to the Church.

"Oh!" said Munyaka with deep emotion. "I am longing to meet my Bridegroom. Are you, too, ready and longing to meet Him?"

One of the other speakers produced a box with a closed lid to represent the heart of man. Every person present was attentive as he opened the lid and drew out one by one things that were hidden inside to stand for evil thoughts, adulteries, thefts, covetousness, deceit, the evil eye, blasphemy, pride, and foolishness—which *Mwathani* (the Lord) said defile the heart of man.

Among those who watched and listened was Mulungit, a shamefully backslidden Masai chieftain who had been an outstanding Christian witness during the pioneer mission days in the Masai tribe. He had accepted the elders' invitation to come to Kijabe and had taken the long journey from Masailand. He was so deeply moved that in the evening he told the elders he wished to make a confession before all the people the following morning. A hush stole over the whole assembly when the well-known Mulungit got up to speak.

"There are many hidden things in my heart which I wish to bring forth into the light," he began, displaying some trinkets of witchcraft. "Here are some charms I bought from the witch doctor to give me good luck. And this one I bought to protect me from sickness and the evil eye. In my heart are hidden away many of the things the preacher of yesterday mentioned. Evil thoughts, adulteries, theft, lying, covetousness, drunkenness, wickedness—they are all there. Today, my brothers in Christ, I call you to witness that I bring these evil things from this dark heart and ask the Saviour to forgive me and wash me white."

Mulungit sat down and covered his eyes with his hand. Johana stood and raised his arms.

"Let us pray to our God of mercy and love to hear the cry of His child and forgive and cleanse," he said and poured out his heart in prayer for one whom he had known for many years.

"This conference," I said to Johana, "reminds me of the way

sunshine bursts forth to roll away the heavy rain clouds at the end of the long rains."

"*Tiitheru, nigwo* [of a truth, it is like that]," he replied with a radiant smile.

Delegates from Kinyona had been at Kijabe for the conference. Theirs was a flourishing Christian center in those days. Great changes had taken place, however, since the withdrawal of the resident missionaries. At first the Christians had felt orphaned, but Sampson Mwenja, our cook of bygone days, then married and settled at Kinyona, was an aggressive Christian with strong qualities of leadership. He had become the acknowledged, though untrained, pastor of the Kinyona flock. He and his elders conducted their church and school affairs, becoming the first self-governing church in all that large district, although they were allied to Githumu station.

Some of the little girls of Warimwe's Gathukiini outschool, for whom we feared when they were taken from school to be forced through the circumcision rites, were married and living with their Christian husbands at Kinyona. Indeed, they belonged to the backbone of the women's group at the church there.

Just before leaving for furlough a few months after the big Kijabe conference, I was invited to spend a Sunday among my old friends at Kinyona and speak to them at their morning service. I felt profoundly the inspiration of the hour, for I had taught many of these people from the time that they indicated their first desire to leave the path of Kikuyu darkness to walk in the path of God. I knew that the Seed sown in some hearts was being scorched by heat and that a crop of thorns of the cares of this world was choking out the Word in the hearts of others before me, so I spoke to them with conviction and purpose, while the Spirit of God drove home the truth of His Word.

Muthungu, who was back in the Kinyona school again and much engrossed in educational and political affairs, sat on the platform among the church elders and community leaders. His head was bowed, his eyes closed. Presently his head dropped lower and he was grasping it with both hands as tears streamed silently down and dropped to the floor. Could he be thinking of that day when he walked in the bushes and made his decision to follow God in His path all the days of his life? Was he confessing to his Saviour how far short he had come from the ideal he had set for himself in that day?

As the people were leaving the church, Njiri came up the path, followed by members of his council. He had been informed of the *Bibi's* coming and invited to be present at the morning service, but the foxy old chief knew the Word of God would prick his heart if he came in time for the meeting.

"*Bibi,*" he said, waving his hand toward the familiar ridges, "they tell me you are leaving Kikuyuland."

"Yes." I laughed. "I am going home to tell the people of America how I helped Chief Njiri to rule these ridges."

"*Tiitheru* [of a truth], is it so?" chuckled the tribal elders.

"But will you not return?" Njiri asked.

"Perhaps so, perhaps not," I replied. "My mother is ill. I have been sent for to look after her as long as she lives. Who can tell if I will be able to return? But you have heard how the Lord *Jesu* came to this world to make a way for us to fellowship with God and has returned to His Father's abode to prepare a place for all who believe on Him. We shall surely meet again in that place if you give yourself to Him."

Chief Njiri took my hand and shook it in the old Kikuyu way. Tears filled his eyes. Was he thinking of that morning in the village school when he was led up to the point of decision and found the way of the Christian too costly for him to tread?

"*Thie na uhoro* [go in peace]," he said abruptly and turned to lead his councilmen down the path.

Woman of Kikuyu grinding meal

Kikuyu woman
carrying
string bag
and baby

Wambui who escorted the *Bibi* to the villages to learn Kikuyu

Thaiti and family standing in front of missionary residence, with Muciri who taught in Kinyona school

Group of refugee girls at Githumu

Miriam teaching carding and spinning of wool

Bibi Truesdell with first teacher-training class

Entrance to Kijabe Girls' School

Making girls' uniforms outside of sewing room

Hospital at Kijabe

Bibi Truesdell with Miriam and family, and Dr. Blakeslee

Mucai, wife, and family with Dr. Blakeslee

Johana
in later life

Johana and Keige

Chief Njiri

British Official Photo

GITHUMU II

1946-1954

Chapter 28

A CHANGED KIKUYULAND

THE TRAIN JERKED TO A STOP at Kijabe railroad station. From the window I could see some of the mission buildings up the hill in the distance, among them the familiar outlines of the girls' school. Was it possible that eight years had elapsed since I had torn myself from that place of joys and sorrows? As we jolted off again and sped on toward Nairobi, I wondered what new encounters there would be with the powers of darkness in Kikuyuland, for fellow missionaries had written of the increasing unrest.

The field director met me at Nairobi, and I learned that the immediate furlough of the two lady missionaries at Githumu would leave *Bibi* Truesdell there alone, so I was to work with her. *Bwana* Teasdale was in Nairobi and would be going to Githumu the following day for his routine quarterly trip as district superintendent. Could I be ready to go with him?

We got a late start as the *Bwana* had many affairs of business in Nairobi. Darkness settled over us long before we reached the last ravine and descended to cross its river and climb to Githumu on the opposite side. It was all home ground, but something was strange about this African night. I missed the hunting call of the hyenas, so incessantly familiar on the ridges. Not a howl was to be heard even though we were not far from one of their notorious haunts in the hillside caves. The station was dark and quiet when we arrived, but the three *Bibis* were waiting up for us with a warm welcome.

The bright sunshine of the next morning revealed many additions to the old landscape. There was a large stone chapel, three houses, a good hospital building, new dormitories and classrooms for the boys' and girls' elementary schools, and a manual training shop. By nine o'clock the teachers and evangelists from the outdistricts began to arrive and collect around the *Bibi* Truesdell's house. She had the oversight of them, and this was the time when *Bwana* Teasdale met all the African workers of the district. They came to greet me, but I sensed a change from the old spontaneous spirit of good will and friendship. At the noon meal that day, the missionaries discussed some of the current problems. The old, experienced officials they said, had been called away to war duty and the whole tribe was out of hand. They spoke also of difficulties among the mission district elders regarding rotation of office. A close-knit clique had fought any change in the *status quo.*

A few days later Isaiah Mucina, the elder brother who had spanked Miriam and sent her back to Kijabe Girls' School after the walkout in 1929, came to the mission house on an errand.

"Have you seen Chief Njiri lately?" I asked him.

"*Tiitheru* [of a truth], he is over there on the ridge right now in the midst of a palaver."

"I should like to greet him."

"Come," he offered, "I will take you to the place of the palaver."

It was only a short walk to the clearing where Njiri sat in solemn conclave with his elders. The formalities of a Kikuyu *cira* (court case) were flexible as to interruptions, so I waited nearby on the ridge path while Mucina entered the clearing.

"*Eha* [where is she]?" I heard Njiri ask Mucina, and immediately he got up and left the group.

"Have you indeed returned to Kikuyuland?" he asked, extending his hand for the old Kikuyu handshake.

The greeting was warmhearted and sincere, but how different Njiri looked! His regal furs and bead ornaments had been replaced by the clothes of the white man. It was only one of the many outward changes in Kikuyuland that I had observed already as I had met the crowds of people coming and going to one of their large markets.

"Where are the *anake* [the young warriors] and the *airetu* [the young girls] dressed in red paint and goatskin garments?" I asked Mucina when Njiri had gone back to his *cira.*

"They are not found in Kikuyuland today. Everyone wears clothes—all but some of the old women and elders."

"I do not hear the hyenas at night. What has become of them?"

"The Government put poisoned meat through the bushes for them. They ate it. Those that did not find the meat ate the hyenas that died of poison and they finished themselves off."

"I do not see any people with yaws ulcers."

"No," replied Mucina, "the Government has opened dispensaries. They have trained Kikuyu dressers to give the people free injections. Very few people with yaws disease are in the villages now. Some affairs in Kikuyuland have changed for the better, but other changes are not good. The affair of the independent schools and churches, pulling the people who once followed the teachings of the mission schools and churches to leave and follow their teachings of *maheni* [untruth], is bringing much trouble to Kikuyuland. Soon you will see that even the mission outschools are very changed from the ones you left."

Churches and schools during the thirties and forties had become popular. Bush schools—independent and mission—were scattered all over Kikuyu territory. The organizations of the independent movement were running real schools at this time, some of them covering grammar school. In the late 1930's Peter Koinange, a chief's son who was considered in the early days to be a genuine Christian, had been graduated from Ohio Wesleyan University in America, received his M.A. degree from Columbia University, and returned to found the Kenya Teachers' College at Githunguri, which was designed to feed teachers into the schools of two Kikuyu independent associations and similar schools to be opened in other East African tribes. At first this institution did not show up as antiwhite even though it was openly independent. The Kikuyu Central Association, before it was banned for subversive activities at the beginning of World War II, had given the college its active support, and Jomo Kenyatta, former secretary of the K. C. A., had succeeded Peter Koinange as its principal, having received a liberal education in London and Moscow.

By this time the Kenya Government was subsidizing mission schools as well as running many of its own and was assuming supervision of educational work. The spirit of nationalism in the independent schools was so strong that they would have nothing to do with the subsidies and thereby dodged inspection by the Government, which unsuspectingly left them alone, encouraged to see the Kikuyu making strides at helping themselves with such commendable educational efforts. Now in 1946 all Kikuyuland was education-mad.

"What," said the younger generation, "young Mugikuyu and unable to read!"

Muthungu was still an aggressive leader in the educational field and was teaching at our Icici outschool on the edge of the forest. He came to see me soon after my arrival at Githumu.

"And how is your school at Icici progressing?" I asked him.

"We have a full school and there is much work. We need more teachers."

"What are you giving in the way of Bible instruction?"

"*He, kai,* do we have time for that? The Government schedule gives us so many things to teach in one day, by the time we get over it all and give the required time for sports, the time is finished."

"But there is a period on your Government schedule marked 'religious instruction,'" I reminded him.

"The morning is gone by the time we cover the work of the other subjects."

"Do you mean to tell me, Muthungu, that you are not giving the children of your school Bible instruction?" I asked, shocked. "Was it not the verses you learned in the bush school at Kinyona when you were a small herdboy that opened the eyes of your heart to see your need and the way of salvation? Do not tell me you have no time to teach the boys and girls of your school the Word of God. I am sure *Bibi* Truesdell has given you all a schedule of Bible instruction to follow."

"All of the outschool teachers have the same trouble. None of us has time to follow it," he insisted, somewhat annoyed that the subject should have come up.

"One thing I will say to you, Muthungu, if you teachers forsake the foundation on which all of these outschools were founded, you will come to grief."

"Many changes are taking place. All Kikuyuland is thirsting for knowledge and to progress like other people of the world. Do we not all wish to do our part to help them?" he argued.

"That is commendable, but I must remind you that God's method of helping a people to progress never changes. Make your Bible period to be the first on your schedule, and you will have time for it."

"*He, kai,* has the Government not put arithmetic on for the first period in the morning?"

Two weeks after the *Bibi* Truesdell and I were left alone, I went to get some cash from a heavy chest bolted to the floor of my bedroom, where the mission funds were kept. The large padlock fell apart in my hands, and when I lifted the lid, hundreds of shillings were gone! Investigation proved that the thief was a former houseboy of the departed *Bibis.* He had unlocked the house door, broken the padlock, and gone off with the cash a few evenings before while I had been teaching a Bible class at the other end of the station.

"What a shock I have had!" I exclaimed as I told *Bibi* Truesdell what had happened. "In all the years I have lived in Kikuyuland, I cannot remember ever having missed one rupee or shilling. Everything I possessed was guarded most carefully by those in my employ."

"Yes, but you know my boxes were broken into, too. All Kikuyuland is disorganized and lawless."

It was not long before *Bibi* Truesdell came in from a safari with another significant piece of news.

"The Fort Hall agricultural officer and his wife came along yesterday while I was inspecting the school at Githima," she said. "He is a fine man, interested in teaching the Agikuyu to contour their ridges to prevent soil erosion and many other better methods of agriculture. When they were told last week to turn out to receive instruction, one thousand of them went to Fort Hall and surrounded the District Commissioner's office by way of protest."

"We are living in difficult days," I sighed. "I have just heard very sad news of another kind. Githae was found dead in his house with an empty alcohol bottle nearby."

Githae was the bright, promising boy who had gone off for advanced schooling with Muthungu, Waitara, and Hanna Nyambura. He had lost two good Government positions because of drink and lately worked as a timekeeper for an up-country settler. After her training at the Pumwani maternity center, Nyambura had done excellent work at the Fort Hall and Nairobi Government hospitals. She came to see me one day at Githumu.

"It is a long time since we last met," I reminded her. "Well do I remember the day you stood, a very small child, shivering at my kitchen door. Now I hear you are to establish your own maternity center in this district."

"Yes," she replied, "I am tired of hospital work. I want to settle down in a village. I have built a house on Mucai's land near his village. The maternity center will be near it. I have a garden, too. See, I have brought you some of my first beans."

"The children of the district where you have built are very neglected," I suggested. "Perhaps you and Naomi *wa* Mucai can gather them together in a Sunday school. You had great skill in teaching the children when you lived at Muthithi with Naomi and Mucai."

"*Hibi* [perhaps]," she replied, not very enthusiastically, rising to go.

"Hanna Nyambura is not the warmhearted Christian she used to be," I remarked to the *Bibi* Truesdell in the evening. "I wonder what has happened to her."

"She is sad over the death of Githae for one thing," answered *Bibi* Truesdell. "For years he urged her to marry him. She hesitated to do so because of his drinking, and Mucai would not hear of it or accept the dowry."

Two of the elders appeared at our house about this time and announced that they had a *ndundu* (a private affair) with me. They led me to an abandoned hut on the mission grounds, where they bade me sit down on a stool while they told me the affairs of their hearts.

"We want to tell you," began one of them, "that the *miceni* [mission] has been telling us to elect two new elders to our council and they want two to retire. We want to explain to you that this is not a good affair. The other men in Githumu are not wise. Those of us who are now members of the council are the only ones who understand our affairs of school and church."

It was very evident that these elders had misunderstood the plan, which made retiring elders eligible for re-election. I tried to explain the wisdom of having a number of elders trained in the ways of the council in case of one dying or moving away, but I could see they were not impressed with my remarks. I sensed some hidden meaning to this whole affair and that they wished me, ignorant of the motives, to stand with them in their decisions.

Another shock was in store for me after I had returned from taking a difficult emergency maternity case to the Fort Hall hospital, thirty-six miles away. I sat by the fire in the evening reviewing the events of the day. Gacau, who had driven the car of a colonel through the Madagascar mud during the war, had been called to drive us over the red Kikuyu roads that had been turned to a mass of mud, ruts, and water by days of steady rain. It had been a nightmare of a trip and I had been terrified lest the poor woman die on the way, yet Gacau had risen to every difficult occasion and the Lord had gotten us to the hospital in time and home again in safety. As my heart went out in thanksgiving to Him, I heard a low, "*Hodi,*" on the veranda and opened the door to find a tall slim girl with a tragic expression on her face. Her light coat and dress were rain-soaked. It was Naomi, Kihoga's young daughter, but what trouble could have brought her out on a day like this?

"Come and sit down by the fire," I told her. "Have you walked from Kinyona in all this heavy rain?"

"Yes, I was sent by my mother," she said, her voice trembling. "We have had great trouble and sorrow in our village this morning."

"Tell me what has happened."

"For a long time the man in the next village and *Baba* [Father] have had trouble over the boundary of our gardens. His cows continually ate the food in our gardens. They have had many words. For the past month he has been making his *panga* [garden knife] very sharp. When the men asked him why he was making his knife very sharp, he said he was going to kill a person. His wife and children were very frightened. They thought he meant to kill his wife, because they quarrel very much and he beats her often.

"This morning *Baba* went to the *duka* [shop] to drink a cup of tea with his friends. As he came down the path from the *duka* to our house, this man jumped out of the bushes. He cut off *Baba's* arm. When *Baba* cried out and turned to go back to the shop, he cut him again on the back of his neck. The men from the *duka* ran out to help him, but when they reached the place, *Baba* was dead and the man was gone. Chief Njiri called the *askari* [police]. They have taken the body of *Baba* to Fort Hall. Oh, *Bibi, Maitu* [Mother] sent me to tell you to come," cried Naomi, burying her head in her hands.

I was stunned. Could this have happened to Kihoga, my first African boy, who had protected and helped me over many a long, weary safari, who could suggest a solution to every difficulty, who had been my stand-by at Kijabe hospital and headman at the girls' school? Nothing of the kind ever had been heard of among the peaceful, law-abiding people of Kinyona. Could it be possible that I was hearing the truth? The sight of poor little Naomi sitting near me, the picture of sorrowful despair, caused me to draw myself together and face the reality.

Kikuyuland, indeed, had changed!

Chapter 29

THE WOMEN TAKE A HAND

BEING LEFT ALONE with all the affairs of a full-fledged mission station during a period of unprecedented restlessness that had made both Christians and pagans unbalanced in their outlook was a tremendous challenge for two women. It was no time for us to sit down and wring our hands and bemoan the ominous trends of the new Kikuyuland. While the *Bibi* Truesdell pursued her numerous duties in the schools and outschools, I was busy with other responsibilities. The native hospital, girls' dormitory, Bible classes, and women's and girls' district and station work were my field.

The hospital which had grown out of the crude affair in which I had struggled with makeshift equipment and universal superstition during pioneer days still had as its head dresser Samuel Muirigi, who had been one of the first to volunteer his services for medical work. A bright, happy Christian, he was patient and sympathetic with the sick, a constant joy to me, and a never-failing helper. Some notable recoveries had been wrought by the Great Physician. A popular maternity ward took care of many mothers. A sullen, indolent spirit among the African nursing staff had given way to one of happy co-operation. There were frequent opportunities to deal with patients about the value of eternal things, and their response was encouraging.

A glance at the work as a whole, however, revealed a shocking lack of Bible instruction. The all-out demand for education minus Bible was disheartening. Caught in the wave of gross materialism that was sweeping the masses before it, former spiritual leaders had left the service of Christ for good-paying jobs and positions of authority. Spiritually minded teachers were scarce, whereas the mission schools had been the means of bringing many of the young to Christ and of giving them instruction in the Scriptures. In the face of such a situation, there was a double urge to fulfill the commission which the Lord had given me before leaving home—to teach the Word.

At the beginning of the first new term after my return to Kenya, I was invited to take up a series of Bible lessons with the church elders, members, and pastors, and also with the boarding girls and boys of the primary school. This was followed by an invitation to teach the women and dormitory girls. Sunday Bible classes with the children began to grow in interest, too. The women were encouraged to meet in their local centers once a week for reading of the Word and prayer. Delegations from the eighteen Githumu district centers met at a given center once a month for fellowship and prayer. It was after one of these meetings, which had become times of blessing and reviving, that the women got stirred up over the spiritual needs of the children.

"*Kai, uhoro uyu ni atia* [what kind of affair is this]?" burst out the indignant Anna, a Christian mother who had been trained at Kijabe Girls' School, now living at Muthungu's school near the site of the old Icamuguthi school on a ridge above Kinyona.

"*Wa ki* [of what]?" asked Eunice, the wife of Warimwe from whose school at Gathukiini the parents once had snatched a promising group of girls to force them through the circumcision ceremonies.

"That the teachers of outschools do not have time to teach the children the words and the affair of God in school. *Kai,* where did they hear the good words of salvation? Was it not at school?" stormed Anna.

"*Tüitheru* [of a truth], the affairs of Kikuyuland are *kurogoco* [a mix-up]."

"This affair of driving the white people away—let the menfolk drive those away from our land who have taught us the way of God, and you will see what trouble will come over us."

Little did our group realize that day how prophetic were these words, nor did they dream of the sorrow that awaited Eunice when, one evening a few years later, she would visit the home of Ngoni and his wife, and a bullet fired at Ngoni by the Mau Mau terrorists would go through her mouth and make her a lifelong sufferer.

Messages went out in all directions to former Kijabe Girls' School girls, now presiding over Christian homes in Githumu district, to meet at Githumu to pray and plan for the opening of Sunday schools for the children of the outschools. What a day of rejoicing it was when they met! There was Anna from Icici and Naomi from Gathukiini. For a long time Naomi had been gathering the children on Sundays to teach them the words of God. Now she was to have lesson pictures and helps. There were Wanjiru and Njeri and Ngabuya, also of the first Gathukiini girls' class. Helen Wanjiku and dear Ruguru came from Ndakaini, Dorkasi from Kamanyaka, Helen from Ruathe. The Sunday schools were opened, and for a year and a half they flourished. The first Saturday of each month the women came to Githumu for four lessons and pictures to illustrate them. They organized the more backward women of lower Githumu district and chose the strongest Christian women from there to open Sunday schools to teach the children the Word of God.

"*Tüthern* [of a truth], the women have much strength in their hearts. We are going forward in the things of God," said Alice of Andrew. "It is the men who have lost interest and are going backward."

"When I returned to Kikuyuland," I remarked to *Bibi* Truesdell some time later, "I was amazed to notice the widespread use of Kikuyu fables by Africans in giving Gospel talks. Since we have introduced studies in the Old Testament characters and events, I have noticed they are using the Old Testament stories instead. There has been a famine of the Word of God in these ridges for some years. I am convinced that the urgent need of Africa today is not for missionary planes to fly over the ridges or for missionary motorists to rush from ridge to ridge, but for missionaries who are willing to settle down quietly to teach the living Word of God.

Soon after the Sunday schools were started, a women's conference convened at Kijabe for four days. The women came from all directions, eight hundred strong. It was a never-to-be-forgotten experience of the presence and work of the living God in our midst. Full of blessing and the inspiration of this conference, the Githumu women began to talk of a conference of their own, which materialized in 1947. The place that was chosen was Ndogomano, one of the largest outschools of lower Githumu district. The school there was large and flourishing, but the church was weak and about to die out.

The conference was held on the very spot where I had camped with the Kinyona schoolboys on that memorable safari when Kambogo, then chief of the district and one of the bitterest opponents of the Gospel, had offered me his little finger instead of his hand in greeting.

"Do you remember," asked one of the evangelists now, "how you said then, 'Does Kambogo think that by offering me his little finger in greeting, he can prevent the Gospel light from flashing out over his ridges to bring salvation and deliverance to many who sit in the prison house of darkness?' "

It was here that vicious hyenas had charged our camp by night and Kambogo had opposed us by day. That was in 1917. Now in 1947 the stirring opening message of the conference was delivered by the daughter of Kambogo, a beautiful Christian woman, the brightest light for Christ in all that district. In spite of the opposition of the powers of darkness through the years, the Lord by His Spirit had called out a people for Himself.

Large crowds met for the morning meetings on the shady slopes at Ndogomano. Mary, a Kikuyu woman who had been saved on an upcountry settler's farm and who had a real message, was invited to come as one of the speakers. God spoke to hearts. In the early afternoons the men, women, girls, and children met in separate groups. An impact was made on the entire community through evening village meetings. The lukewarm elders from the various outchurch centers were stirred.

"We are ashamed," they confessed. "We are supposed to be the head of affairs. Compared with these women and their zeal, we are few in number and weak. If these women should take the wooden sticks they use to mash their cooking food and come at us, they would overcome us. If being a woman means doing this kind of work for the Lord, it would be better to be a woman than a man."

"Some of us are like bees," commented Joshua Mugo, the faithful leader and saint of Kamanyaka church. "People speak to us. We fly at them and sting them with words. We have come here to have our stingers removed and to be healed of our stings. We have not been able to withstand the enemy because of broken shields. We have come here to have them mended that we may return to war a good warfare."

About the time of the Ndogomano conference, the *Bibi* Wingerd, a first-term missionary, had come to Githumu to take over the schoolwork so that the *Bibi* Truesdell might go on furlough. Not long after that, we began to hear reports of a new movement abroad in the schools of Kikuyuland. It originated with European physical culture teachers in the Government schools who wanted to "preserve the good" in African customs.

"Here is a letter from the Government Educational Department," announced *Bibi* Wingerd one day after reading her mail. "They want one or two of our teachers to be sent during school holidays to a school center in the district where instruction in physical culture is to be given to teachers. One object is to preserve the best of the tribal dances and songs."

"These Government women teachers ask various Kikuyu teachers and leaders to give them a list of 'good' dances and songs. Some of the leaders are independents. They are sure to capitalize on the ignorance of these European teachers by introducing songs that have only immoral objectives in view," I replied.

One of the most talented of the Githumu teaching staff was sent to comply with the order. He returned to teach the boys and girls daily during the physical culture hour that which he had been instructed to teach them. Before long an unbridled back-to-paganism spirit was apparent in our station school. At the same time plans went forward for a great sports' day in August, 1947, which was to include all schools of the district. Githumu station was selected as the place to hold it. It was an embarrassing predicament for the missionaries, yet there was little that we could do to oppose a project that had an almost united African front in its favor. However, we could, and did, resort to prayer—and it was the African Christian women whom the Lord raised up to put a measure of restriction on the program.

Alice, one of the most spiritual women of Githumu district, stood to her feet in the women's meeting.

"*Tiitheru* [of a truth]," she began, "*Cetani* is designing many affairs to try to deceive us and pull us back into the dark paths we have left. We hear now about a sports' day. Do you not hear the Githumu schoolgirls dancing every day? Are they not being taught to do exercises that are immodest and lead to evil thoughts? Are they not being prepared to do these exercises publicly and to dance before crowds of men spectators who will gather to watch and choose the winners of prizes? *Kai,* did not we, their mothers, forsake these same dances and evil ways of Kikuyuland to walk in the path of God? Do we want our daughters instructed in mission schools to walk in the path of darkness we have left?"

"We do not," responded the women with one accord. "We will oppose this sports' program to make money for the schools."

Then the Christian women arose to speak their minds to the elders, husbands, fathers, and teachers. The hearts of the men were stabbed with conviction. Certain of the most offensive numbers were struck off the sports' program. Independent schools competing were forbidden by the African judges to produce them. The sports' day started with crowds, streaming banners, and band music. One event began to follow another amid much applause. Then God sent a heavy downpour of rain. The crowd scattered, tried to return, but finally left. Financially the day was a failure. God dealt with the elders and head teachers over the matter. All the school children then were commanded to go to the Sunday school classes.

Chapter 30

UNDER THE RAINBOW

THE YEAR OF 1947 was drawing to a close. Once again, as in 1929 to 1931, the Agikuyu were in the sieve. On the one hand, there was a movement of the Spirit of God that knew neither church nor tribal boundaries. Groups of people throughout our own Kikuyuland tribe were being gloriously saved and quickened. They had a great love for the Word of God. Feeding on and delighting over its contents, they would sit by the hour reading it together. They were willing to come out from the lukewarm, backslidden masses, and when forced to do so, they were willing to walk with Christ without the camp, receiving the same kind of treatment He was given. On the other hand, the forces of darkness were consummating their long-planned strategy and setting their battle lines for the final showdown against the forces of light which they could not tolerate in their usurped domain and against which they had plotted since the appearance of the first beam of heavenly light in their midst.

During the years of World War II, it had become necessary for the Government to ban the old Kikuyu Central Association because of its subversive activities and to intern its leaders. The ban on the organization never was lifted even though the end of the war in 1945 had led to the release of its detained leaders.

However, a new political association already had sprung up with far greater coverage than the old one. It was known as the Kenya African Union, had administrative headquarters in Nairobi, and claimed as its purpose the unification of the progressive elements of the many tribes into a body which would bring about better conditions for all Africans of the Colony. Members of the banned society had flocked to the new one. Its leaders soon rose to prominence there, and it was not long before Jomo Kenyatta, who had been the general secretary of the K. C. A., was president of the K. A. U.—so that the two organizations had one identity in the minds of the Agikuyu even though the K. A. U. consistently denied any connection between them.

By the end of 1947, although the ostensible motives of the new association were not such as to create undue suspicion, a a storm of unprecedented proportions was gathering underneath, and once again the Kikuyu tribe was the storm center in Kenya Colony. The storm clouds were rolling heaviest over the districts of Githumu and Fort Hall, casting dark shadows over many who had professed to be subjects of the Prince of light, even those who had dared to forsake the paths of heathendom at great cost in days gone by. For a year or more the church services at Githumu had been filled with women and children, but the men were conspicuously absent. Political intrigues consumed most of their time as they met in the coffee shops, townships, and trading posts now scattered throughout Kikuyuland.

We had observed all this with apprehension and already had felt some of its reverberations—among our mission schoolteachers when they dropped the Bible classes from their schedule and made every pay day a nightmare by their demands for higher wages and equipment entirely beyond our means to furnish, among our church leaders in secretive attitude and spirit of independence without a willingness to shoulder the responsibility of complete self-support—but we had no inkling of the true state of affairs until the morning that a note was delivered to us while *Bibi* Wingerd and I were at breakfast.

"What do you think of this!" I exclaimed, and began to read aloud.

> You missionaries have done good work during pioneer days. We are grateful for what you have done, but now we ask you to leave Githumu district. We wish to carry on. We have sent copies of this letter to the District Commissioner, the Director of Education, the field and home councils of the Africa Inland Mission.

The letter was signed by the leading teachers and elders of the district. It was a shock to see the signatures of men with whom we had labored in the Gospel for many years, yet so strong was the spirit of nationalism abroad in their land that few Agikuyu were unaffected by it. The letter was the forerunner of a series of violent outbursts which we could not have believed possible among our church constituency. The missionaries had attempted to prepare the Africans for the spiritual leadership of their people and expected to vacate when they had a sufficient number of qualified, balanced leaders to carry on. But they did not believe that the Agikuyu had reached that stage of development. Therefore, we were prepared to stand against what we felt to be an opposition from the powers of darkness, using deluded and misguided Kikuyu teachers and elders as instruments to bring to pass their purposes. The second blow was struck when we paid no attention to the letter but carried on as usual. It came almost immediately and was directed at the December women's conference which was about to convene.

"*Hodi kwa Bibi,*" two familiar voices called the Kikuyu equivalent for knocking at my bedroom door one Sunday afternoon. The guests who had come to call were Alice and Naomi, wives of two Kikuyu pastors.

"We have come to ask if it is not time to send the notice of the date of our women's conference to all the centers in the district," they said after exchanging greetings. "Tomorrow is market day. If they were ready, we would take them to market and send them out from there by people who come from all the outschools."

"So it is time," I replied. "I will type the notices if you will wait."

"This conference will be the largest women's conference we have ever had at Githumu," Alice and Naomi said triumphantly as they left with the bunch of envelopes tucked away in their bags.

The following day two solemn church elders came up the path and called me out of my house for *ndundu* (a private word).

"We have been sent to tell you there will be no conference at Githumu," they announced. "The women are not allowed to meet. The notices will not be sent to the market. Instead, Andrew has been sent to market to spread abroad the report to all the centers. There is to be no women's conference. *Ningi,* also we have been sent to tell you that all the Sunday schools the women teach are closed, too."

"Come up on the veranda," I said to the elders. "I want to give you *ndundu* [a private reply]. Do not forget that I am in Kikuyuland because the Lord *Jesu* said, 'Go ye . . . and teach all natons.' Do not tell me these words you have been sent to give me. Go and tell them to God. The battle is His. Go in peace. My words are finished."

Except for the fact that the women were not allowed to meet any more with the missionaries but were told to carry on their meetings independently, nothing more of significance occurred on Githumu station until February. A Sunday morning service had been dismissed, and the congregation stood about in groups on the level green ground exchanging news. After pleasant greetings, we missionaries looked from the doorway to discover the people seated on the grass by the church. A leading elder was standing in their midst speaking excitedly, pointing a finger in this direction and that to emphasize his points. Not a word leaked out as to the nature of that meeting, but it soon became apparent that there were those who had determined to lead out—by arguments, threats, fear, Utopian promises, or any other means at their disposal—the Githumu church membership from the guiding hand of the mission to place itself under African leadership alone.

Men such as Joshua Mugo at Kamanyaka were a strength and blessing to us at this time. One of the first converts and the outstanding saint of Githumu district, he was persecuted for righteousness' sake as few have been. Open insult was his constant reward for loyalty to true Christian principles, yet he never returned evil for evil.

"Joshua Mugo has been brought to the hospital. He is very ill," said Muirigi one morning in February when I reported for duty at the hospital.

Nothing but surgery could save his life, so we called Gacau and set out for a quick trip to Fort Hall hospital, but five miles from Githumu, Joshua's head fell forward and his spirit departed from Kikuyuland. Wonderful to hear were the testimonies given at his graveside by those who had been helped by him in times of trouble!

"I do not wish him back in the midst of our trouble, but where will we find another champion and warrior to lead us?" asked a brokenhearted member of his Kamanyaka flock.

"The fragrance of a life hid with Christ in God remains," I said. "All the present strife and hatred have been more than this gentle, kindly soul could bear."

We missionaries needed a special message of hope in the strife and hatred that surrounded us, too, and God was pleased to write such a message in the heavens for us. It was on a Sunday afternoon in the middle of March after a light shower.

Bibi Wingerd at one end of the station, and I at the other saw it at the same time. Each of us stood transfixed as we beheld the largest, widest, most brilliant rainbow we had ever seen. It was bowed over the missionary dwelling and the African girls' dormitory, touching the earth at both ends. It seemed to warn us of impending danger, but also to assure us of God's protecting presence with us.

About this time, the *Bibi* Mathys, just back from furlough, joined us at Githumu and took charge of the primary school while *Bibi* Wingerd continued in the secondary school. A new wave of antagonism was breaking upon us. A secret opposition party with high-powered propaganda was organized in the district. Its leaders petitioned Government to call a meeting of Africa Inland Mission and Government officials to meet at Githumu. The local Agikuyu, they said, wished to take a vote as to the Mission's continuing its work or turning it over to the Africans. The District Commissioner, being a fair-minded man and not knowing the background for this move, set the date for the meeting—April 6. We heard that propagandists were working day and night to gather ten thousand Agikuyu from all parts to march to Githumu to vote the Mission out.

The staff at Githumu knew this was a spearhead attack. Ground gained or lost at this point would affect all mission work in Kenya. There we were, a small band of helpless souls against an enemy ten thousand strong. We appealed our case to the Lord of glory, remembering the rainbow, and were prepared to trust His methods. The first day of April came, then the second and the third. It was only three days before the crisis day. That afternoon a Government order was broadcast to the people through the chiefs that there would be no meeting at Githumu on April 6. Instead, Mission representatives and selected Africans were invited to meet Government officials at Fort Hall on April 29.

The outcome of the meeting with Government representatives at Fort Hall was an announcement that the mission station could not be closed nor the missionaries expelled, and an invitation to the people of the district to co-operate. Thus thwarted in their plans, the opposition resorted to more violent methods. At the beginning of the May term of school, the African staff seized all the schools of the district and station, including equipment and fees, and students were ordered to walk out of the classroom if a missionary teacher entered. At the same time, the hospital was boycotted and emptied of its patients by agitators who entered it as visitors. Africans were forbidden to sell food to missionaries or any Africans who were loyal to them, and the order was enforced. Cries of distress from a small boy were heard from the direction of one missionary home on a Sunday morning when all who would go to church were in the midst of a service. One of the men went to investigate.

"One of the rebels rode up to your house on his bicycle," he reported to the missionary when he returned. "He took the milk bottle from the Kamanyaka boy who brings your milk. He poured out the milk and broke the bottle, and he has beaten the boy. He asked him if he did not know all Agikuyu have been forbidden to sell any food to the white people and the black people who refuse to leave them. *Kai,* is it not a very bad affair!"

There was an exodus of backslidden church members who compelled many of the true ones to go with them under threats. A Sunday morning service in progress in the station church was interrupted by the ringing of the church bell and the small band of faithfuls forced to give place to the opposition group to hold a meeting of its own. Thereafter each group occupied the building at a different time on Sunday. School was carried on with makeshift equipment in one of the hospital buildings for the few who dared to stand against mass opposition.

As for our food supply, God still had His ravens who were

quick to do His bidding. One of them was a slight, bent, old Kikuyu granny who appeared at the door one day loaded down with a chicken, yams, bananas, and milk. She was the mother-in-law of Joshua Mugo.

"Why, Gucu, where have you come from!" I exclaimed. "And how did you reach Githumu? Did the people along the way not stone you?"

"I have come from my home at Kamanyaka. Yes, they threw sticks at me and told me to return to my village," she replied, her black eyes snapping. "I asked them if they thought Gucu would allow the people at Githumu to starve when she had food in her garden? Did they not know the *athungu* [white people] did not refuse to help me or them when they were sick? I ran right along, and the sticks did not harm me."

"Come into the kitchen and rest," I said to her when she had unloaded her baskets on the veranda. "You shall have some hot tea and some sugar to take to your village. We have never had a friend like you, Gucu."

"Joshua would have brought food to you if he had been here. Now that he is gone, I will bring it. I do not fear the stones of the Agikuyu," she returned.

Week after week old Gucu loaded her bent back and came to us with food. A church elder from one of the outschools, hearing of our plight, also braved the jeers and threats of his fellow tribesmen to bring us vegetables, fruit, milk, and eggs. A lorry brought us supplies from Kijabe. Our temporal needs were met.

This condition prevailed until the end of June, when another conference was called at Fort Hall and the Government took a hand again. All church and school equipment and supplies were ordered left intact. The school fees were to be returned. The Mission was to resume its role of directing the Githumu station schools. The day following this conference, the rebel teachers were dismissed and the pupils sent home to learn their fathers' wishes concerning their return. A few days later, both schools were opened with a staff of African Christian and missionary teachers, which included the *Bwana* and *Bibi* Miller, of Kijabe, and was conducted on definite Christian principles with Government educational standards. Thus they continued to the end of the three-month term with a reduced enrollment. The outschools, however, never came back under missionary supervision.

Relief was brought in the church situation when the Government persuaded the opposition party to build their own meeting place. They put up a mud and wattle structure just over the boundary of the mission station and registered themselves as the African Christian Church. But we had not seen the end of violent outbreaks. One night in October I was awakened at one o'clock by the flash of a powerful light in my bedroom and the noise of someone tampering at my window.

"*Mukwendatia* [what do you want]?" I called sharply.

There was a sound of retreating footsteps. I got up and blew my police whistle. The blasts brought *Bibi* Mathys and several African girls from the next house to investigate, but all was quiet by then. My housegirls were called to sleep in the living room and we settled down once more. Two hours later we were awakened suddenly again.

"*A-o-u-! a-o-u-! a-o-u-!*" the cry of alarm was coming from the hospital.

The noise of breaking glass came from the same direction as windows in the night nurses' room and delivery room were shattered. I arose and lit the lamps, but remained in the house, somehow restrained from going out, while others went to the hospital. After another two hours, the Millers' house, the African teacher's, and boarding-school cook's houses were attacked, but no damage done beyond the breaking and removing of the locks on the doors.

In the morning the evidence around my house enabled us to

piece together the story of the night. Heavy stones from the retaining wall near my bedroom window had been removed and broken. No doubt a gang had planned to smash the window and enter, but their plans had miscarried when they found the window protected by expanded metal. The many footprints that were found in the garden behind my house led us to believe that, failing to force an entrance to the bedroom, a gang had waited there, using the commotion at the hospital as a ruse to draw me outside.

"This was exactly the procedure used twenty years ago when criminals removed a rock from the retaining wall back of Hulda Stumpf's bedroom, smashed the window, entered, and took her life," I said, looking at the loose stones, and as I spoke I remembered the rainbow which had been bent over the missionary home and the African girls' dormitory.

European police and detectives who had arrived immediately to investigate this outbreak reported the troublemakers to be local young men and schoolboys backed by opposition leaders. When the leaders failed to bring the culprits to him by a specified time, the District Commissioner sent six armed African police to take up quarters on Githumu station for three months and made a levy on the people of the district to pay their wages. Thus plot after plot was laid and crisis after crisis, when there seemed no way out, came and went—but Githumu station quietly carried on all of its activities in the usual way, the Lord working with His servants.

By the time the first school term of 1949 opened, there were more students than could be accommodated. All those who remained through the crisis passed their Government exams. We praised God with full hearts for the primary and secondary Christian schools operating on a firm Christian foundation, schools which continue to the present day on the same basis and full to capacity. Once more it became a joy to meet the classes in their Bible hour each morning, to observe the keenness with which they responded, and to look forward to the day when they would go forth to be the mouthpieces of God to the Kikuyu people.

Chapter 31

TERROR ON THE RIDGES

IT WAS THE TIME OF THE MONTH when the moon does not rise over the ridges of Kikuyuland—in August of 1952. All the villages were shrouded in darkness. Fear clutched the hearts of many villagers as they sat about their fires speaking to one another in subdued voices.

"The oath-givers came out from Nairobi on the taxi[1] today. They are hiding at Gakarara independent school. A Mugikuyu told me they will take us all to their oath-giving place in Githutha's village tonight," whispered a young man to his old father.

"*Tugiike atia, tiga tweterere* [what can we do but wait]?" asked the old Kikuyu elder, taking a pinch of snuff to steady his trembling limbs.

"If they come tonight, it will be very bad. Two Christian women and Wangeri, the daughter of a Githumu pastor, are sleeping here on their way to a meeting of the people of God."

Suddenly out of the darkness they heard cries of distress from the opposite ridge and then the voice of a man singing. The words rang out clearly in Kikuyu:

Precious Saviour, Thou hast saved me,
Thine and only Thine I am.
Oh, the cleansing blood—

[1]The bus of East Africa.

The song ceased abruptly, and there was silence.

"*He, kwa Ngugi, nimanyitatwo* [in Ngugi's village they have been seized]," said the young Kikuyu, retreating to the inside of the hut.

At Githutha's village the stage had been set. In the large *thingira* [the men's hut], an arch had been constructed of banana trees and branches with long thorns. Impaled on the thorns were eyes that had been gouged from various sacrificial animals. Beneath the arch on the skin and intestines of the sacrificial ram was a large gourd propped up by stones to keep it from tipping. It was filled with a mixture of blood, bits of meat, and the contents of the stomach and other organs of the ram. Around the large gourd shell were smaller ones containing earth to represent the Kikuyu loss of land, blood, and revolting portions from the body of the animal. The eyes of a sheep glared from two long thorns planted in the earthen floor at either side of the arch.

A large group of Agikuyu had been rounded up in their villages like cattle and driven to this diabolical place. They stood outside the *thingira* waiting to be admitted one by one, questioned, instructed, and warned by the evil-looking oath-administrators. One of the Christian women who was on her way to the meeting of the people of God was snatched roughly from the crowd, pushed into the *thingira* to stand before the gruesome paraphernalia, and made to pass through the arch.

"You will take the first oath of secrecy," ordered the oath-giver, while his assistants drew her blood and smeared her body with it as he forced some of the vile contents of the gourd shells into her mouth. The vows, with their curses, were repeated over her:

> I will not divulge the secrets of this society, or this oath will kill me.
>
> If I see anyone stealing anything from a European,

> I will say nothing, but I will help him, or this oath will kill me.
>
> If I am told to bring in the head of a European or of my husband, I will do so, or this oath will kill me.
>
> I will obey all the orders of the leaders of this society, or this oath will kill me.

When these and the rest of the vows that composed the oath had been solemnized over the unwilling woman, she was warned of what would happen to anyone who reported the night's doings to the authorities and then pushed, dazed and trembling, from the *thingira,* while Rose-Mari Wangari, the daughter of the Githumu pastor, was shoved inside to stand before the ram's eyes and go through the arch. Smearing her body with the blood and filth of a gourd shell, the oath-givers forced some of the meat into her mouth.

Wangari bowed her head, threw up her arm, and shot the mouthful of meat into the folds of her dress, claiming as she did so the cleansing blood of the Lamb of God. The men began to repeat over her the same oath, other requirements of which were:

> Swear:
>
> That there is no God but the Kikuyu god.
>
> That the Bible is the white man's lie.
>
> That you will help us close mission schools and drive the Europeans from our land.
>
> That you will refuse to work for the white man.
>
> That you will not refuse to take the life of anyone you are told to kill.
>
> That you will return to practice all Kikuyu customs.

On and on through the hours of the night this process continued as unwilling victims went through the ceremony that bound them to secrecy and acts of violence. Over on the next ridge, where Ngugi had been dragged from his house to be brought to the oath-giving arch, his song, "Precious Saviour, Thou Hast Saved Me," ringing out in triumph in the night air, had frightened his captors lest they be discovered. They had silenced him with a blow on the head, and when he fell heavily into the bushes, they thought they had taken his life and ran on to his Christian brother's village on the next ridge. There Marion, who was in the bedroom surrounded by her sleeping children, and who soon was to give birth to another child, was seized and pushed and pulled along the path toward the village where the oath was being given. Fainting and falling to the path, she, too, was left for dead.

In the morning a note was brought to me by a secret messenger from Ngugi's brother, who was Marion's husband.

> Help, in the name of the Master, help. We have poured two five-gallon tins of cold water over Ngugi's head, and he has revived. Marion also lives. Come for us.

The mission car was dispatched at once to take them to Fort Hall hospital, which we found crowded already with similar cases. When the Government was appraised of what had happened to Ngugi and Marion, we were told to take the matter to our local chief to be dealt with.

"But," I sighed, when this word came, "Chief Mwangi will do nothing."

While we had been enjoying a breathing spell after the prolonged upheaval at Githumu, a sinister movement had been making rapid headway, working under cover of the Kenya Africa Union and the independent schools and churches. It was the secret society of Mau Mau, led by Jomo Kenyatta and other Kikuyu fanatics, whose goal was to capture the support of the entire Kikuyu tribe, presenting themselves as its supernaturally appointed liberators from European oppression. Their aims included the reclaiming of all land occupied by the white man, the driving out of all foreigners, the destruction of Christianity, and the restoration of ancient customs along with the extension of modern education. With wild exaggerations of the land grievances and Utopian promises of great progress under self-government, it had not been difficult for these leaders to gain an ardent following among the discontented and nationalistically minded element of the tribe. Their operations, however, were to remain secret until they were strong enough to accomplish their objective by one mass uprising.

With this end in view, they skillfully built up an intricate organization which got representatives into key positions all over Kikuyuland, set about collecting supplies of firearms and ammunition, and began an intensive training program for its leaders. Its members gained control of the various independent schools, which were turned into Mau Mau indoctrination centers, chief among them the independent teachers' college at Githunguri. For over twenty years these schools had been engaged in raising a generation of potential terrorists. One of the most successful pieces of propaganda was the widespread use of "hymns" which denounced the white man, challenged the people to rally to the interests of the Kikuyu tribe, urged them to deeds of violence against all enemies of their cause, extolled the leaders of the K. A. U., and derided the old Kikuyu elders. At first these "hymns" were passed on orally, but later they were published in a succession of books. Most of them were sung to the tunes of familiar Christian hymns and some of them were extremely blasphemous parodies, substituting the name of Jomo for the name of Jesus Christ and proclaiming him as the saviour of the Agikuyu. For a long time their significance went unnoticed by Europeans, few of whom spoke Kikuyu and thus took them for bona fide Christian hymns.

Once the people were convinced that Mau Mau had something to offer them in providing a solution to their economic problems, it was not difficult to persuade them to contribute funds and to take the first oath of membership which bound them to secrecy and absolute obedience to their leaders but revealed little of the true character of the organization which they were joining. The membership ceremonies in which they took part were a strange combination of those which accompanied the time-honored Kikuyu practice of legal oath-taking, of their solemn tribal initiation rites, and black magic, plus a little perverted Christian phraseology. They would not dare to go back on such an oath for fear of supernatural reprisals, and this fear was reinforced by threats of what would happen to anyone who dared to betray the organization.

The second oath committed members to definite actions and sometimes was combined with the first oath, which might be taken for the participant by a sponsor and still be as valid as though he had repeated the oath himself. There were several higher levels of oaths, which could not be spoken by a sponsor and led deeper into the inner circles of Mau Mau, accompanied by unspeakably degrading acts at some of which the members balked when they realized what they were getting into. However, threats usually were effective, and once taken, the oath was binding. No one who refused one of these advanced oaths was allowed to get away from the ceremony alive, for the organization could not afford to have anyone loose with such knowledge unless he was committed to its cause.

In the early days of the movement, the chief recruiting grounds of the Mau Mau had been among the Kikuyu squatters on the upcountry settlers' farms, although the administrative headquarters were in Nairobi. It was in the middle of 1950, during the brief period when I was stationed in the white highlands after the arrival of reinforcements at Githumu, that rumors of the oath-giving ceremonies among the squatters began to trickle through and the existence of the organization became known. The inability to continue in secret caused Mau Mau to intensify its efforts and to use force to bring the people under its control, depending for security on the superstitious fear with which the Kikuyu regarded an oath once it was taken. This accounts for the fact that, even then, its activities did not create any widespread alarm or arouse suspicions that would cause Government to consider it dangerous.

However, by the time I returned to Githumu early in 1952, the atmosphere had grown very tense. When the masses of the Agikuyu in the native reserves had become aware of what was going on, they were shocked, and Mau Mau was meeting with opposition from two unexpected sources. Whereas great numbers of nominal Christians had fallen easy prey to their tactics, genuine believers not only stood against the movement, but if they were forced through the ceremonies, they did not fear supernatural punishment for breaking the oath, and were likely to go straight to the authorities to report what had happened to them. Also some of the old Kikuyu elders, who considered the Mau Mau to be an outrage of their ancient customs, and oaths taken under the present conditions invalid, set about to stir up their people to resist the movement. In May the first great mass ceremony denouncing Mau Mau and calling upon the Kikuyu people to rise up against it took place in Nyeri district. This was followed by similar demonstrations all through the reserve.

Mau Mau retaliated with a wave of counterdemonstrations and an outbreak of such deeds of violence as never before had been witnessed on the ridges of Kikuyuland. Their objective was to terrorize the tribe into subjection before the opposition could thwart their plans. Mau Mau gangs were operating now in the villages all about us, and no one was safe from their ruthless attacks. Many took the oath in self-defense in order that they might go about their daily business unmolested. A few Europeans were the victims of foul murders, but the greatest part of the violence was being directed against the loyal Kikuyu true Christians especially being subjected to brutal treatment, for while Mau Mau appeared on the surface to be a subversive political organization, in reality it was nothing short of a diabolical religion. It was the culmination of the master strategy of powers of darkness which they had been developing since pioneer days to reclaim their subjects and blot out forever the light of the Gospel of Jesus Christ on these ridges.

The Government made a few arrests but was unable to prosecute the perpetrators of the atrocities because anyone known to have taken information to the authorities was murdered, or simply disappeared, leaving no one to bring definite evidence against the accused or to lead the police to the hangouts of the gangs. However, there were some, especially among the Christians, who were willing to risk their lives in order to reveal what they knew of the operations, objectives, and personnel of the gangs in order to put a stop to the terror in their midst.

The mettle of the Christians was being tested again as it was in 1929, but this time, instead of an exodus from the house of God, there was an increase in church attendance in Kikuyuland. Pastors braved journeys to outlying places to minister to the spiritual needs of the Christians there and to preach the Gospel. We saw the iron enter into the souls of those who walked in the path of God and saw them prove the reality of the faith that was in them.

Soon after Ngugi had recovered from the treatment received on the night of the oath-taking at Githutha's village, he read the Word of God with his family before they prayed in the morning. The verse that fastened itself upon his memory was, "The name of the Lord is a strong tower: the righteous runneth into it and is safe."

About four o'clock that afternoon he and his brother were riding their bicycles from the trading post to their nearby village. There was a flash of fire and a report from the roadside bushes.

"*Jesu!*" cried Ngugi, as a bullet whizzed by his head.

There was another flash of fire.

"*Jesu!*" he cried again.

Four bullets whizzed by, but Jesus was his strong tower, and Ngugi rode home in safety.

Many of the Christians had to face the enemy in their own homes. One day a frightened woman came to *Bibi* Boda. She was one of the leading Christian women of Githumu.

"May we come to sleep on the floor of your house tonight?" she asked. "My son with violence insists every night that we go to the oath-giving village."

That night the floor of the Bodas' living room was the bed of refugees. During the following evenings, Christian refugees from many directions flocked in to fill every available space in the girls' dormitory.

As the situation got more and more critical, three loyal senior Kikuyu chiefs went on a tour with Government officials to the upcountry farming areas to arouse the Agikuyu to a realization of the dangers of becoming involved in the Mau Mau movement. They told them it was a bad affair and begged them to return to co-operate with Government to forward the progress of the Kikuyu tribe. One of these men was Waruhiu, a beloved, highly respected Christian chief. The others were Chief Nderi, and Chief Njiri, who had retired a short time before but was called back into service because of the seriousness of the crisis and the wisdom he showed in dealing with his people. On October 7, soon after their return, Chief Waruhiu was shot in his car as he was returning from a district meeting. The following week the Home Guard was organized, composed of loyal Kikuyu who acted as an emergency patrol force.

It was at this time that Chief Njiri stepped up on my veranda followed by an armed guard.

"They have shot my friend Waruhiu," he said with emotion. "I receive many letters from the Mau Mau to warn me they will take my life, too."

"We are living in dangerous days," I replied. "It is time to get right with God."

"Are you protected by soldiers?" he asked, disregarding the spiritual warning in his characteristic way in spite of his friendliness and concern.

"They are at the chief's camp," I told him.

"That is too far away."

"But who will tell them to guard our station?"

"I will. I am the ruler of this district. Do not be afraid, *Bibi.* Mau Mau can do nothing to you. They cannot." And with this he left.

A week later Chief Nderi was hacked to pieces when he attempted to break up a large Kikuyu gathering. Of the three chiefs, Njiri alone remained, and a close armed guard was put around him day and night for his protection.

"They will get him, too," predicted many. But would they?

By the end of October a state of emergency was declared in the Colony, which enabled the Government to take quick and drastic measures. Almost immediately came the arrest of 130 top Mau Mau leaders, including Jomo Kenyatta, who, after a long drawn-out trial, was sentenced to seven years of hard labor on the northern frontier of Kenya. The teachers' college at Githunguri was closed, as were all the independent schools, for they had become oath-taking centers. Before another year had passed, the K. A. U., which had become completely indentified with Mau Mau, was banned. Large detention camps were set up, in which to detain all who were arrested for their connection with Mau Mau, and in time these camps were filled with many thousands of men, as well as a number of women.

The arrest of the top leaders of the organization did not materially affect its efficiency of operation, for, as it was discovered later, all of them had deputies appointed and trained to carry on their functions. At the beginning of the emergency, the Mau Mau moved into the great forests of Mount Kenya and the

Aberdare to train an army. They operated a wholesale recruiting system in Nairobi for the army in the forests, had a well-developed intelligence system, and continued their oath-taking ceremonies and raids from there. Thousands of head of cattle were wantonly destroyed. The atrocities committed became more and more gruesome as the hunted Mau Mau got increasingly desperate for funds, arms, food supplies, and a following—for they had no intention of abandoning their diabolical project. Was not *Cetani* behind them in a frantic attempt to rid Kikuyuland of any possible source of heavenly light, and had not his wrath grown bolder with each new decade of encroachment upon what he had considered his impregnable domain?

It was not long before a strong police headquarters established on our mission station border was busy hunting and mopping up Mau Mau adherents. It was in this police camp that the people of the little Christian community where Ngugi had his village found refuge, for the Government brought them here to live for their protection.

In this atmosphere, with soldiers, raids, and arrests all about us, the work of Githumu station continued—hospital, schools, church services where the flock needed comforting and sustaining during the dark days of sorrow, Bible classes, ministry to refugees. As we trusted in the Lord for our safety, we gave Him all the praise for the privilege and power of carrying on in quietness and peace of heart. From time to time it pleased Him also to give us tokens that He was keeping that which belonged to Him on the ridges.

Someone from a back seat touched my arm at the close of a meeting during our November conference, and I turned to see the smiling face of an old man.

"I felt I must come to greet you," he said, shaking my hand warmly. "You and *Bibi* Collins taught me the way to God at Kinyona when I was a young man living in heathen darkness.

I have always walked in that way. I will never leave it. Abide with peace."

"Is the *Bibi* here?" called a familiar voice outside my door about the same time. It belonged to my old friend Paul Njuguna, a pioneer teacher-evangelist of Githumu.

"I could not leave Githumu until I had come to greet you," he said. "Do you remember the safari we took down to my father's village when all these ridges were in the darkness of evil spirits?"

Paul always liked to recall that safari. He went on to remind me once more of how we had told the people the way of life and light, how the chiefs and elders had opposed us bitterly, how his sister as a result had been among the first seven Kikuyu girls to leave the paths of darkness and come to Githumu station to be taught, how she was now the wife of a Christian man and one of the Githumu women who still walked firmly in the path of light.

"I am an old man now. And, *Bibi,* you are old, too. But it does not matter that we grow old. We have done our work. *Cetani* cannot uproot the Seed we sowed on these ridges. Remain with peace," he finished as he bowed, smiled, and turned toward his faraway village, calm in the Lord in the midst of the terror abroad on the ridges.

Chapter 32

ACHING HEARTS OF KIKUYULAND

THE YEAR OF 1953 was a year of much sorrow for the people of God on the ridges and of aching hearts throughout Kikuyuland.

Simeon, the son of a Kamanyaka church elder, was one of the schoolboys who had refused to join the walkout in 1948 and had followed the *Bibi* Wingerd to continue his studies in the makeshift schoolroom in the hospital building. He had finished teacher training at a Government school and was a brilliant teacher on the Githumu staff at the beginning of the Mau Mau attacks.

"Simeon came home this morning more dead than alive," *Bibi* Wingerd told me excitedly one morning in January. "He went yesterday to greet his family in his father's village. A boy he thought to be one of his best friends betrayed him to the oath-giving Mau Mau operating in their district. They seized Simeon in his father's village last night and drove him with other victims to the oath arch. He was the last to be taken to the arch at the break of day and was stiff from sitting out in the cold night air. He refused to obey their commands. His eyes are bloodshot, his body a mass of bruises."

"*Bibi,* the Mau Mau brothers of my husband came to our

village to kill us all," cried Ruthi, the daughter of Joshua Mugo, bursting into my living room on a Sunday morning some time later.

Ruthi had been one of the girls in the first teacher-training class at Kijabe Girls' School. Now she was the wife of a Christian teacher in one of the outdistricts. They lived in an isolated section, and he had to be away from home for his work during the week.

"We have escaped," she went on. "I have left my children in my mother's village at Kamanyaka. Will you bring them to Githumu?"

At this time Muthungu was employed by the African Christian church as a teacher at Githima, which had been a Githumu outschool until the breach had come. When he and others of his organization saw the true character of the subversive movement, they registered their loyalty to Government and supported Chief Njiri. Their action was highly commended by Government officials, who took great pains to sponsor and give grants-in-aid to their schools. There were some unique opportunities to give these people help, but even though they were disillusioned regarding the trend of political affairs and had not gone back to polygamy and other pagan customs as other independent church organizations had done, they never were reunited to us.

Mau Mau now considered Muthungu an enemy to their cause. On his way back to his home at Kinyona from his school one Friday afternoon, he was seized by a band of Mau Mau. A terrific battle followed in which he was overpowered, battered from head to foot, bound, blindfolded, and thrown into a thicket far removed from calling distance to any passers-by. He lay there helpless until an early hour in the morning, when a gang returned to push and drag his almost helpless body to the oath-giving village. There bits of the sacrificial meat were forced down his throat and he was left in the bushes to die.

Slowly and painfully Muthungu crawled to a main road where he was picked up by a lorry and taken to Fort Hall Government Hospital. For months he lingered there, a mere skeleton of his former self. These were months of quiet time, far removed from the hectic round of committee meetings, arguments, strife, and sedition that filled the land—time to think, time to reflect on the promises made to God when he stood on the threshold of life. Muthungu came out of the hospital much wiser for his sad experience.

One Sunday afternoon toward the end of February, all the villages on the ridges and in the valleys were abuzz with excitement. Young men on bicycles were being dispatched in all directions. A beer drink was progressing at the trading plot near the mission station. The African *askari* (soldiers) were being "tanked up" for a purpose. Leading oath-administrators and Mau Mau executives from Nairobi had come in for the occasion.

"Bring in by force the men, women, and children of the district who have not taken the oath," they commanded the young men they had sent off on the bicycles.

The missionaries at Githumu station felt the oppressive atmosphere charged by the powers of evil operating all about them. About four o'clock word came of what actually was taking place.

"Tell the *askari* to come to the mission station at once," said a missionary to a boy who was sent to deliver the message.

Later three *askari* staggered up the path to the mission house.

"*Jambo* [greetings]," said the missionary. "What is going on?"

"*Wa-wa-wa,*" mumbled one *askari* as he stumbled and fell to the ground, his rifle flying from his numb hands in the opposite direction.

One of the other *askari,* confused and stupid from drink, tried to collect the rifle. Succeeding after a struggle to stand uncertainly on their feet, they ambled back to the plot mumbling to themselves.

On Monday a British officer, looking for a place to quarter a platoon of the King's African Riflemen, which they wished to bring into the district, asked permission to bring the platoon to Githumu station. Within a week the platoon, with their European officers, had taken up quarters in the Githumu primary school buildings and pitched their tents on the surrounding green.

It was about this time that we got word of two of the Matara elders having been called out of their village by terrorists with a gun. They were taken to the forest and nothing was heard of them until long afterward, when their torsos were discovered in a deep hole.

One Sunday in August, when the Githumu pastor had been called away, Onesimus, the evangelist, was asked on short notice to give the morning message. Onesimus always was ready with a message on short notice, for constantly in his spare moments he was pouring over the Word. The many Githumu schoolboys and girls as well as the adults listened with rapt attention. They always listened thus when Onesimus spoke to them.

"A Mau Mau gang from Kamanyaka ran after Onesimus to take him to the oath arch. They have been sent to compel him to take the oath or to take his life. He has refused to take the oath and has escaped from them more than once. *Kai,* is he not in danger?" whispered one Githumu Christian to another.

The next Sunday morning Onesimus sat in the audience when Bible questions were asked from the platform. His answers rang out clear and correct. From the service he went with his schoolboy son to a crude little coffee shop nearby for a scone and a cup of tea. The gang, in search of their victim, seized him by the throat.

"Pray, pray to your God that He may save you!" they cried, mocking him.

"You refuse to take our oath, do you? Who are you to refuse to obey the words of the Agikuyu? What do you have to say now?" they demanded as the blows were delivered thick and fast.

"I go, I go to live with *Mwathani* [the Lord]," he answered with his last breath.

The long sharp knives of his brutal tribesmen dismembered his body. His head was buried in a thicket by the river, his other members in different places. The remains of his son were carried near the river to be covered loosely with thick leaves. Police on the trail of the gang discovered it a few days later, but the whereabouts of Onesimus' body was a secret for a long time.

Months later, when a local member of the gang was captured, he was forced to confess the fate of Onesimus. He led African Government police to the site where the head had been buried. The skull was tied about the neck of the criminal, and he was taken to court to confess his crime and give the names of his fellow gangsters.

Tiitheru (of a truth), sorrow filled the hearts of the Githumu Christians. But was not the head of John the Baptist presented to a ruler's wife on a large platter?

"No one knows who among us will be the next," they said, "but what says the Word of God? If we believe that *Jesu* died and rose again, even so them also which sleep in *Jesu* will God bring with Him . . . then we which are alive and remain shall be caught up together with them in the clouds. . . . Wherefore comfort one another with these words."

Over on the Mununga Ridge billows of smoke rolled heavenward early one morning in the latter part of the year. From Githumu we could hear the rapid firing of machine guns. Heavy bombing planes flew over the station in the direction of the forest. Awe-stricken men came from Kinyona to the hospital speaking in low tones and holding their hands over their mouths—a Kikuyu gesture expressing great consternation and deep emotion.

"The head of Thigiru, Njiri's favorite son on whom he depended to execute his orders, has been brought to the chief's village," they said faintly. "Njiri is very angry. He sent all the Home Guards and the King's African Riflemen stationed at his village to Mununga to kill every man on the ridge. The men of Icamuguthi and Gathukiini, hundreds of them, are lying all about the villages and in the bushes dead. Their villages have been burned. Their cattle and sheep have been taken. Their gardens have been destroyed. The women and children have fled to caves and thickets to hide.

"Njiri sent Thigiru to direct the digging of contour ditches to teach the people better affairs of planting gardens. They refused to dig them. A gang of Mau Mau men from the forest were hiding in a thicket when Thigiru went to carry out his father's orders. They overcame him. Njiri says all the people on Mununga Ridge are Mau Mau and helped to kill his son. We have never seen affairs like these in Kikuyuland. We are overcome by fear and sorrow."

"Have you any news of my old herdman, Thiga, who lived at Mununga?" I asked as I thought of the many people in the outschool districts there that I had known and taught.

"His village is destroyed. His cattle and sheep have been taken. His *kiimba* [carcass] probably is lying there unburied with the many others," they said with a shiver.

"A man from Kinyona was admitted to the hospital today. His name is Gacingiri. He says you are a friend of his," the missionary nurse told me as she passed my front door some days after the destruction of Mununga Ridge.

"Yes, he was one of the boys in my catechumen class at Kinyona."

An hour later my cook carried a pot of tea and slices of bread into the men's ward while I followed behind. Gacingiri and his teacher had not met for some years. Our greeting was warm-hearted and cordial.

"Do you know the *mwanaki* [young man] in the bed opposite?" he asked as we talked together.

"Have I ever known him?"

"Is he not Kariuki, the son of Thiga? He had been working on a farm and was on a visit to his father when their village was destroyed. He fled to the bushes and was overcome by malaria for many days. He was weakened by sickness and lack of food, but he crept to the road leading to Thika. The new chief of Githumu found him by the roadside and brought him here."

I went over and spoke to the *mwanaki* in the opposite bed.

"Is it true you are Thiga's son? And your father, is he alive?"

"All the Mununga men are missing. Many are dead. Some may have escaped."

Ten days later a tall, thin Kikuyu woman came up the path from the hospital to my house. Her skin was rough and covered with rash from exposure, but her head was high and her spirit unbroken.

"Is not this the *Bibi* who lived at Kinyona?" she asked. "Did I not bring you *ndoma* [dasheen] from my garden when Thiga herded your cows?" she asked.

"Are you the wife of Thiga?"

"*E-e-e* [yes], I heard my son Kariuki is in the hospital. I wept when I saw him. I thought he was dead."

"Is Thiga with you?"

"I know where he is," she whispered.

In a few days she came back again with Thiga.

"Oh, *Bibi!*" he exclaimed as he collapsed in the grass, buried his face in his hands, and wept while his wife sat down beside him.

"Bring them some tea with much sugar," I called to the cook and then turned back to Thiga.

He was a pathetic figure, weak and weary from exposure and the terrifying experience through which he had passed. The ridge where his prominent landowning clan had lived was devastated. His cattle were gone—the fine part-European cattle had been the idol of his heart.

"Oh, and their *big* udders! They were like this," he wailed extending his arms to show me how big.

How different might have been his outlook now had he opened his own heart to the Light of life when he asked for a teacher of the words of God to open a school in his village in the pioneer days at Kinyona!

"*Nimukurara guku* [will you sleep here]?" I inquired of these two, full of pity for their plight.

"We do not know."

All available space was already filled with refugees, but the girls were called to clear out a cookhouse and bring bundles of dry banana leaves for beds on the floor. By sunset Thiga and his wife were sitting beside a crackling fire listening to the welcome sound of a boiling cookpot.

"Is he eaten by his teeth?" I asked Samuel Muirigi as I stopped beside him and offered up a silent prayer of thanksgiving for this faithful hospital dresser, remembering the pioneer days when the people had come to me in preference to the Kikuyu "dentists" who pried an aching tooth from its bony socket with a garden knife.

Muirigi was poised, forceps in hand, before an old man sitting on a grassy bank pointing to the tooth that was "eating" him.

"This old man has come from the refugee camp between here and Kinyona," he said. "Government has gathered together all the remaining people they can find in the bushes of Mununga Ridge along with many refugees from the upcountry farms. They have overseers to take them out every day to cut brush. They are paid enough cents to buy the day's supply of cornmeal. We hear the Government leaders say surviving members from Mununga Ridge will never be allowed to reclaim their land. All of that district is to be used for hospital and school sites. What have these people to look forward to? Even if they are released from camp, where will they go? When these children are grown, where will they find gardens to cultivate?"

The heart of Muirigi was wrung with sorrow for his people as he looked at the old man, a representative of the multitudes in camps.

"Hanna Nyambura is in this camp, too," he continued. "She was in Nairobi hospital many months because of an infected hand. Now that she has returned, the district about her maternity center has been evacuated, and she spends days in camp as a refugee."

"The love of material gain has brought Nyambura down to this," I said. "She must know that God is dealing with her. Will she return to the place of blessing and fellowship with Him?"

Chapter 33

FAREWELL TO THE RIDGES

WE HAVE HEARD IT SAID that you are going back to your land," Pastor Wanduru said to me one day as the eventful year of 1953 was drawing to a close.

"Eight years have come and gone since I returned to Kikuyuland," I replied.

"But we do not feel you have finished your work," he protested.

"Wanduru," I said, "if you knew how I feel at the close of the day after descending many times to the girls' dormitories and domestic science rooms and back to my house, you would know that I have finished my work."

When the news got out that I was leaving Kikuyuland for good, it brought a steady stream of farewell calls and invitations. Muthungu and Wambui came down from Kinyona. They spent the night at Githumu, and we had a long visit the next morning. Then I took them in my car up the road toward Kinyona. We stopped on the site of the old Mathanjiini outschool, where two large beautiful dormitories and the foundation for a third had been built. It was being done by Government and was to be named the Njiri High School in honor of Chief Njiri, who had been decorated by the Queen for long, loyal service. Now all the building operations had been suspended, and the workmen dismissed because of battles with the terrorists who were operating on all sides.

Muthungu, who was a member of the Government local native council and the district educational committee, took great pride in explaining the layout and plans for the school. Two palatial stone buildings, furnished with modern equipment, were to be the homes of the European principal and vice-principal. The plan called for eight more such buildings to house the European staff.

"To the right of the dormitories," said Muthungu, "is the site for the homes of the African members of staff. All branches branches of instruction will be taught by college-trained African teachers. There will be African teachers of mathematics, history, science."

"And where," I asked, "is the site for the home of the teacher who is to teach the Word of God to these students?"

"I have not heard of a plan for a teacher of this kind, although I have said repeatedly in our council meetings that the cause of our present troubles in our schools is the lack of Bible teaching. I have told all members, European and African, that in order to succeed we must restore the teaching of the Bible to our schedule, and we must have Christian teachers to teach it."

As I listened, I recalled the conversation we had had in 1946 regarding the lack of Bible instruction in Muthungu's own outschool.

"Like all of us," I thought to myself, "Africans learn their most valuable lessons in the school of hard knocks."

On my last Sunday at Githumu, I answered a knock at my door to find two men standing on the veranda.

"We have come from Kinyona on our bicycles," they said. "The district between here and there is closed, but we said we must see you before you leave. If we perish, we perish."

One of the men was Arthur Ngoni, my small houseboy of

the pioneer days, who had called his brother to be my cook. He was one of the Christian stalwarts of Kinyona. Shot at in his home, the recipient of many threatening letters, he knew on whom he had believed and was persuaded that He was able to keep him.

"We have come to send you on a mission," they said. "We are living in a tight spot at Kinyona. We and our families live in barbed wire entanglements. *Will you ask the Christian people of America to pray for us?* Will you greet in the name of the Lord our Saviour all of our friends who in the past have come to Kikuyuland to teach and help us? Could you send us some verses or literature from time to time to help us stand firm?"

"I came to say good-by," said dear Ruguru, who was in the hospital with her sick infant, Ruguru who had been kidnaped on her way from the dormitory to the schoolhouse in the Kijabe Girls' School walkout and taken back to her heathen relatives. Now she was one of the leading Christian women at Ndakaini. Their church, school, and homes had been burned by terrorists from the forest. They had fled with their children, to be delivered miraculously from the knives of the slayers. Now they had returned to rebuild their villages.

"Ruguru," I asked her, "do you Christian women of Ndakaini still meet to pray together?"

She looked into my face with a radiant smile.

"We could never cease to meet to pray and read the words of God together, because they continually threaten us. What can they do to us? If they take our lives, they will but release us from our bodies to go to live with *Mwathani* [the Lord]."

What power could Mau Mau have to destroy a faith like that!

When I left Githumu to spend the Christmas holidays at Kijabe, whom should I meet in Nairobi but Johana. The Government had asked the missions to supply evangelists to live at the Athi River prison camp to help the Mau Mau leaders and terrorists who were detained there to "take a sane view of life for themselves and their tribe." Four had gone from other missions, and Johana had volunteered to make the fifth. More than two years later Keige was to join him at Athi River and share his labors there in the same devoted spirit with which she had stood with him as a faithful helpmeet through all the long tumultuous years since that first Christian wedding at Matara. At this time Johana had been at Athi River for several months and was on his way home to Kijabe to spend Christmas with Keige and his family. The *Bibi* who took me up to Kijabe found a place in her loaded car for him as well. People, black or white, could always make room for Johana.

After we had arrived at Kijabe, we chose a time for a real visit, and Johana turned up at the appointed hour with his old radiant smile.

"Now tell me what you have been doing down at Athi River Camp," I asked him after we had settled down over a cup of tea.

"When I first went down," he began, "the officials said to us, 'All of these prisoners in this camp must be compelled to work.'

"I said to them, 'No, no, we do not want to force them to work.'

" 'Why not?' asked the officials.

" 'Well,' I replied, 'if we use force with them, they will not listen to our words. We want to help them to believe the words of God.'

" 'Have it your way. See how you will come out,' they said."

Johana knew his people, and the Government officials had a high respect for him. His gift of pouring oil on the troubled waters brought the same results in the prison camp that it had brought in the days when God had used him to calm the angry heathen parents of our refugee girls at Kijabe.

"Every morning," he continued, "we evangelists begin to

move about among the prisoners and talk to them. At first they bit us with words and would not listen. We just left them, and went on to talk to others. Every day we talked to them *kahora kahora* [patiently, patiently]. Finally some of them began to listen to our words. After a time we said:

"'There is work to do about the camp for any who want to volunteer to work.'

"*Tiitheru riu* [of a truth now], more than one hundred of the prisoners work, and these are the ones who come and listen well at our public meetings, when we sing and explain the words of God. Ten of these have confessed their sins and been truly saved. The officials believe them to be genuine and have given them responsibilities in the food supply store."

We went on to talk of old friends and acquaintances of Kikuyuland, some of whom had found their way into Athi River Camp, deluded by the false promises of Mau Mau. Johana was to have a fruitful ministry to some of these as well. He spoke that morning of Gacau, on whom we had called many times to drive our emergency cases over bad roads to Fort Hall Government Hospital. Later in the homeland I was to hear how Gacau renounced Mau Mau and came out on the side of the Prince of light, how he was released from detention, and how he himself became one of a group of believers who regularly visited the prison camps to teach the words of God.

"The twelve o'clock bell is about to ring," said Johana as he rose to take his leave. "We have had a good talk about some of the affairs we have seen in Kikuyuland. I return to camp tomorrow. When do you leave?"

"I am booked to leave Nairobi by plane for London, January 16. My boat across the Atlantic is due to arrive in New York about February 4."

"*Wathie* [when you go], *thie na uhoro* [go in peace]," he said.

"*Na we* [and you]," I returned, "*thie na uhoro.*"

Yes, it was possible for me to go in peace a few days later when my plane soared aloft to wing its way over and beyond the ridges of Kikuyuland. The beautiful, fascinating Kenya I had known and loved in the early days was dead, fallen prey to a murderous enemy, but I knew that the God who created Kenya and its people remains unchanged, and that the promised day surely is coming when His righteous rule with healing in its rays will rise and cover those ridges as the morning sun bathes them in its golden light.

EPILOGUE

From my home in America

TO MY FRIEND AND GOOD HELPER JOHANA:

We have had a long safari through Kikuyuland on the business of *Mwathani* [the Lord], since the day we first met at Matara when you were a young Christian and I was a new missionary. Often we have walked together over the ridges and through the valleys telling the Agikuyu of the love of God and the cleansing blood of *Jesu.* Together we have carried poor sick people to the mission station from the bushes where they had been taken to die, and nursed them back to life. We have protected Kikuyu girls who fled to us for refuge when every hand was against them.

In the beginning of our safari through Kikuyuland, we found the people friendly and responsive, but when the light we carried revealed the darkness and evils of their customs, only a few were willing to walk in the narrow path of *Jesu,* and we found ourselves in the midst of warfare. The powers of darkness worked through chiefs, elders, and the *andu ago* [the witch doctors] to discourage us and drive us out. Their power and craft were great.

Take a look at those early days: Twin babies had their nostrils and throats packed with leaves as soon as they were born and were left in the bushes for the hyenas. Kikuyu girls and women spent their lives in toil and bondage. Young warriors in red paint and heathen ornaments danced themselves into a wild frenzy, like evil spirits incarnate. Once in a lifetime, the old men and women adorned themselves as the young and danced the *muthunguci* on the great open spaces until they fell exhausted, in an effort to renew their youth. The unwanted old folk were led to the depths of the forest and abandoned. Diseases for which there was then no cure ate away the flesh of men and women. Cattle and sheep and women were seized by raiding tribes.

Our safari has led us into a new Kikuyu world, Johana. No more does the hyena roam the ridges in search of the dead and dying. The tribes no longer raid each other. Kikuyu girls are protected by law. Only the scars of the gaping ulcers are left. Skilled Kikuyu doctors, compounders, midwives, and nurses in charge of hospitals and dispensaries fill the land. Educational institutions have been established. Kikuyu members sit on the legislative council and help to make the laws that govern the Colony. These changes are good, and some of them have come because the love of God alters man's surroundings as well as his heart.

But, Johana, we are still in conflict with our enemy of pioneer days. His hate is cruel and relentless. In the latter part of our safari, we have faced him in the open with the Mau Mau, who have shed the blood of nearly a thousand of the staunchest followers of *Jesu* and devastated all Kikuyuland. I know that they are still breaking out with deeds of terror and that the spirit which is in them walks on all the paths of Africa. I have heard since I came to America how the progress of ambitious Agikuyu has been stopped, how their businesses have languished, how their large new school buildings have been left unfinished because the Mau Mau war has sent the builders off to fight. I have heard how the village life has disappeared and the flocks are gone from the hillsides and the gardens left untended because the people are in prison camps or herded into great communal villages so that the Government can watch them to prevent their secret feeding of the Mau Mau army.

Because of all this, men are saying, "You have labored in vain. You have wasted your lives. Christianity has failed in Kikuyuland."

You and I know better, Johana. *Mwathani* [the Lord] did not send us to change the whole Kikuyu tribe. He sent us to give them the Light and trust Him with results. But as we and others have obeyed, the Light of the world has flashed over all Kikuyu country. Many have escaped from the clutches of the prince of darkness. The complete Kikuyu Bible is in their hands, and Kikuyu pastors, evangelists, and teachers are ministering to their spiritual needs. They are the Church of Christ in Kikuyuland, and "the gates of hell shall not prevail against it." It will not be long before our Prince of light returns to spell the doom of our enemy. Continue to give forth the word of light through the present darkness, and tell the Agikuyu Christians that the end of the battle is near, when we shall be given crowns to cast at the feet of *Mwathani.*

Yours in faith for victory,

—H. VIRGINIA BLAKESLEE